Happy
by
Design

Happy
by
Design

How to create a *home* that boosts your *health* & *happiness*

Victoria Harrison

aster

For my wonderful parents – masters of the art of creating a happy home.

· ·

An Hachette UK Company
www.hachette.co.uk

First published in Great Britain in 2018 by Aster,
a division of Octopus Publishing Group Ltd,
Carmelite House, 50 Victoria Embankment,
London EC4Y 0DZ
www.octopusbooks.co.uk

Text copyright © Victoria Harrison 2018
Illustrations copyright © Debbie Powell 2018
Design and layout copyright © Octopus Publishing
Group Ltd 2018

Victoria Harrison asserts the moral right to be
identified as the author of this work.

ISBN 978 1 91202 356 1

A CIP catalogue record for this book is available from
the British Library.

Printed and bound in China

10 9 8 7 6 5 4 3 2 1

Publishing Director: Stephanie Jackson
Junior Editor: Ella Parsons
Copy Editor: Zia Mattocks
Art Director: Juliette Norsworthy
Designer: Gemma Wilson
Illustrator: Debbie Powell
Production Manager: Caroline Alberti
Picture Researcher: Jennifer Veall

Contents

The Happy Home Programme

"I set out to try and find the answer to one simple question: Can our home make us happier?"

Everyone wants to be happy, but sometimes we look for happiness in the wrong places. Wealth, power and prestige might bring us a short-term boost, but often it is the simple pleasures in life that can bring the greatest level of peace and happiness.

A relaxed alfresco lunch on a sun-drenched summer's day, the cheerful crackle of a roaring log fire or the quiet peace of your favourite armchair on a lazy Sunday morning; these small moments of domestic contentment are easy to overlook, but maybe we should be focusing on them more in order to boost our wellbeing?

With stress, anxiety and burnout seemingly on the rise, I wanted to discover if we could actively improve our health and wellbeing simply by the way we design our living spaces, and if there were any shortcuts to happiness that we could all embrace. So I set out to try and find the answer to one simple question: can our home make us happier?

My journey into the science of happiness led me to some fascinating places, from the research labs of NASA to the forests of Japan. As I went along I started to build up a universal "Happy Home Programme" with the aim of helping everyone create a living space that heals, calms and nourishes. The resulting book, *Happy by Design*, is packed with tips and inspiration to help you live your happiest life. You can either work right through it, to follow the full wellness programme, or dip in and out for a mini hit of happiness whenever you need it.

By shifting the way we think about our living spaces, from how they look to how they make us feel, I will show you how to create a happy, uplifting home that looks after you from morning to night, and even when you are asleep. Happy reading!

1

How to Grow Your Own Fresh Air

How many plants do you have at home? Perhaps you have a succulent in the living room or a peace lily in the bathroom, maybe a fern gently wilting on a windowsill. But have you ever really given much thought to the impact that these humble houseplants could be having on your health and happiness?

If the answer is no, then it could be time to think again (and show them a bit more love) because choosing the right plants could be one of the smartest things you can do to boost your health and happiness levels indoors. And the good news? If you have already got a peace lily in your bathroom, you are on to a winner.

Apply Some Rocket Science

If you aren't sure exactly why you should have plants in your home but have just always felt that having some around you is fundamentally "a good thing", you will be happy to know that you are on the right track. You are also in the company of some very smart people, because when I started delving into the world of houseplants, my research led me to a rather surprising place: NASA (National Aeronautics and Space Administration).

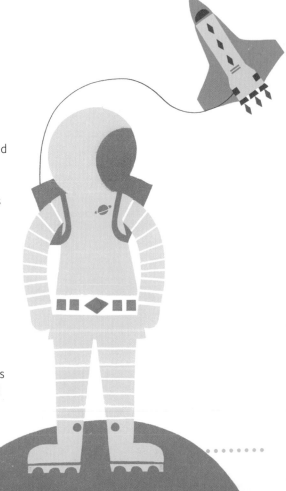

It turns out that indoor plants have been given space-age levels of consideration over recent years, starting in the 1980s when a team of NASA scientists, led by Dr Bill Wolverton, undertook a Clean Air Study to look at ways of tackling the newly observed phenomenon of "sick building syndrome" (SBS). This can occur when a building is sealed too well and pollutants, released by carpets, furniture and even cleaning products, can build up and get trapped inside. Think of it as being inside a space rocket, but without the breathing apparatus.

Get some leafy Zen

SBS has been linked to some pretty unpleasant symptoms, such as headaches, dizziness, nausea and eye, ear and nose irritation, and, if you live in a well-insulated modern home, you could be at risk of it. So, that's the bad news. But on to the good news – did NASA find a solution? Yes, they did and it's beautifully simple: plants! Lots and lots of houseplants.

I asked Dr Wolverton just what plants could do for us. "Research shows that just being in the presence of plants helps to reduce stress, lower blood pressure and, in work environments, increase worker productivity," he says. "Plants also remove airborne volatile organic chemicals (VOCs) and particulate matter." But you might also be interested to know that your houseplants could be giving you a natural mood boost, too. "They emit negative ions," says Dr Wolverton, "which not only help reduce airborne microorganisms, but give us a euphoric feeling."

NASA discovered that the best way to treat your indoor air to a detox is simply to bring in hard-working houseplants. They drew up a list of the top 50 indoor plants for soaking up pollutants, some of which are listed overleaf.

What else can plants do for us?

Several scientific studies have revealed that plants in an indoor environment can also lower blood pressure, reduce stress and impact our overall health in a positive way. Japanese scientist and plant guru Kozaburo Takenaka has spent many years researching just this and developing the concept of "ecology gardens" in hospitals and public buildings. I asked him if he believes that plants can do more than filter the air, and his response was unequivocal: "The ecology gardens not only cleanse the air, but they also bring people peace of mind," he told me. "Indoor plants are needed by everyone in the world who aims for clean air and a healthy life indoors."

Pick a Plant, Any Plant

So, how should you choose which plants to have in your home? I asked Kozaburo Takenaka if there are certain plants that we should all have in our living rooms or particular plants for the kitchen, for example, but his advice was surprisingly simple. "I think it's more important to choose plants that match the indoor environment," he said. "For example, the extent that they match the brightness or temperature of the room they are intended to be placed in. This is highly important for the owner of the plant in order for them to derive maximum satisfaction as the plant grows."

The hot list

The list below illustrates ten of the best performing plants in the NASA experiment. On the following pages we will look at the best plants for sunny rooms and the best plants for shady rooms, as well as highlighting a small group of plants that have an extra-special skill.

ARECA PALM (*Chrysalidocarpus lutescens*) A champion among plants when it comes to removing indoor air toxins, this graceful plant is fast growing and elegant, so suits a bright living room or an open-plan space. The feathery leaf fronds have a soft yellow-green tone and grow in graceful arcs that bring a lovely sense of life and movement to a room.

LADY PALM (*Rhapis excelsa*) Another leafy powerhouse when it comes to removing toxins, the lady palm is rather more slow growing than other palms, so it suits smaller rooms and compact homes. It has thick, glossy leaves that provide a sturdier appearance than the more delicate areca palm and is very easy to maintain so is a good choice for first-time plant owners.

BAMBOO PALM (*Chamaedorea seifrizii*) Elegant and refined, with clusters of slim canes and elegant leaves, the bamboo palm can grow up to 1.8m (6ft) tall, so is perfect for creating a "living screen" indoors, if you need to divide an open-plan room, or for making a soft wall of green in an urban home.

RUBBER PLANT (*Ficus elastica*) One for design purists. The clean lines and sculptural beauty of the rubber plant make it a perfect partner for clean-lined architecture. These beautiful plants can grow very tall, so are good for larger rooms, and they have the added benefit of being fairly hardy, so will tolerate cooler temperatures and shadier conditions than the more delicate palms.

DRACAENA 'JANET CRAIG' (*Dracaena fragrans*) Perfect for livening up a shady corner, this structural plant can grow quite tall and will last for many years if well cared for. The sturdy stems and glossy dark green leaves have a "tree-like" appearance and work well in a contemporary interior.

ENGLISH IVY (*Hedera helix*) If you want to add a dash of refined glamour to your home as well as scrub the air clean, English ivy is the plant for you. This pretty, trailing plant will twist and drape elegantly over shelves or tumble gracefully from a hanging planter, detoxifying the air as it goes.

MINIATURE DATE PALM (*Phoenix roebelenii*) If you want to bring a touch of the tropics to your living room, the miniature date palm is the one for you. Excellent at removing toxins, it has the look of a pineapple tree and as such will bring with it a whisper of hot skies and warm seas to your suburban living room.

FICUS ALII (*Ficus binnendijkii* 'Alii') If you want a tall houseplant with a delicate elegance, look no further than this plant. Hailing from the sunny shores of Thailand, it will appreciate a sunny spot in a bright, airy room. In return it will quietly and efficiently whisk away indoor toxins and purify the air for you year-round.

BOSTON FERN (*Nephrolepis exaltata*) On a par with English ivy, the Boston fern is a very pretty indoor plant that will lend an elegance to any shelf or tabletop you place it on. It will need a little attention – regular misting and a sunny position – but it will reward you tenfold with its excellent toxin removal powers and decorative beauty.

PEACE LILY (*Spathiphyllum wallisii*) In at number ten is the pretty peace lily, an excellent all-rounder that will suit almost any style interior, thanks to its glossy tropical foliage and tall white flower stems. This elegant beauty will be happiest in a warm spot, but it isn't too fussy about light levels, so can tolerate semi-shade if required.

The six best plants for a bedroom

Did you know that the majority of houseplants release oxygen during the day but not at night? So if you want to oxygenate your bedroom while you sleep, you'll need to pick one of a small tribe of plants that go against the grain and work hard to clean the air right through the night. The following plants are all night-time oxygenators that are believed to stand guard over you while you snooze.

Plants that work the night shift

- Aloe vera (*Aloe vera*)
- Dendrobium orchids (*Dendrobium*)
- Gerbera (*Gerbera*)
- Moth orchid (*Phalaenopsis*)
- Mother-in-law's tongue (*Sansevieria trifasciata*)
- Peace lily (*Spathiphyllum wallisii*)

The eight best plants for shady corners

These plants will cope in darker rooms and semi-shady nooks, so use them to freshen up those rooms that get the least amount of natural daylight.

- Arrowhead vine (*Syngonium podophyllum*)
- Chinese evergreen (*Aglaonema*)
- Elephant ear philodendron (*Philodendron domesticum*)
- Golden pothos (*Epipremnum aureum*)
- Heart-leaf philodendron (*Philodendron scandens*)
- King of hearts (*Homalomena wallisii*)
- Red emerald philodendron (*Philodendron erubescens* 'Red Emerald')
- Mother-in-law's tongue (*Sansevieria trifasciata*)

The eleven best plants for sunny rooms

The following plants will be happy in sunny conditions (although be wary of harsh, direct sunlight), so fill a bright, warm room with a selection from this list and watch them thrive.

- Aloe vera (*Aloe vera*)
- Croton (*Codiaeum*)
- Dwarf banana (*Musa oriana*)
- Ficus alii (*Ficus binnendijkii* 'Alii')
- Florist's mum (*Chrysanthemum*)
- Gerbera daisy (*Gerbera jamesonii*)
- Kalanchoe (*Kalanchoe*)
- Norfolk Island pine (*Araucaria heterophylla*)
- Tulip (*Tulipa*)
- Wax begonia (*Begonia semperflorens*)
- Weeping fig (*Ficus benjamina*)

"The best way to treat your indoor air to a detox is simply to bring in some hard-working houseplants."

The Ten Best Ways to Decorate with Plants

If there's one thing that illustrates how fashions move in cycles, it's the current craze for houseplants. The last time they were in vogue it was the 1970s and the chicest homes were filled with woven macramé planters and large terracotta pots housing leggy spider plants and verdant ferns. But as times changed they fell out of fashion, to make way for the more minimal aesthetic of the 1990s. However, after decades in the design wilderness, homeowners are once again waking up to the beauty of indoor plants and I for one, am thrilled. Here are a few ways to embrace the houseplant revival and bring a little leafy drama to your living space.

 Group them

There is something to be said for the power of a group of plants. So instead of placing one lonely little plant on a shelf, try clustering a group of plant pots together for maximum impact. Choose different-sized planters to vary the height, and mix various types of foliage together until you hit on a combination that pleases you. Odd numbers always work better than even ones, so try a group of three or five plants.

2 Dot them along bookshelves

To add life, colour and interest to a shelf, alternate stacks
of books with potted plants for a living, breathing display.
Choose a plant that suits your interior and have fun with
it. For example, trailing ivy (*Hedera helix*) will bring a sense
of grandeur to a bookcase. Or, if you want to showcase
a colourful paperback collection, dot smaller houseplants
along the bookcase in vivid, coloured pots to match the
bright book spines.

3 Hang them from a shower rail

Adding plants to a bathroom can create a fun, tropical feel,
but space is often limited so you will need to get creative. Try
utilizing the shower rail, if you have one; just pop a couple of
hanging planters over the rail and fill them with moisture-loving
plants. I like to loop a small bunch of eucalyptus stems over my
shower rail, too; the steam from the shower releases the
eucalyptus oil into the air and creates a lovely scent that
makes me feel like I am in a posh spa. Try it – it is
surprisingly effective.

Create a jungle

Growing up, I loved the giant Swiss cheese plant (*Monstera deliciosa*) in my parents' living room, and the way it lent a wonderful jungle-like feel to the room – it seemed terribly glamorous to my younger self. If you also like the idea of creating a luscious indoor jungle, the key is to go for volume and layer up a mix of foliage-heavy specimens. Stack them up at varying heights to create real impact – a plant ladder is good for this because it allows you to stagger the plants. Garden centres often stock plant ladders for outside use and you can easily prop one up against a wall in a living room and load it with green plants. Alternatively, try placing a collection of plants on a cluster of small tables of different heights.

Add elegance with an orchid

For a refined interior, nothing beats the beauty of a single, tall orchid. Whether you choose an individual stem and place it by the bed or group a few together for a pretty cluster, the tall stems, delicate petals and rich, glossy leaves will add a touch of class and instantly elevate any room in the home. I like to think of the orchid as the Grace Kelly of the plant world.

6 Suspend them

If space is at a premium, hanging planters are great for adding lots of plants to a small room. Add impact with one large plant or group smaller plants in clusters of three. Lightweight macramé planters are good for hanging near a window, as they won't obstruct the light too much, and they will also bring a touch of 1970s glamour to your living room. Alternatively, to liven up a plain wall or a dark corner, try a mix of brightly coloured hanging planters and suspend them at varying heights.

7 Climb the walls

Wall-mounted plant holders can look surprisingly fresh, if you choose a contemporary geometric shape or a metallic finish. These are best suited to trailing plants and those that don't need much water, so choose low-maintenance plants and encourage them to tumble elegantly from the planter and down the wall.

"If you like the idea of creating a luscious indoor jungle, the key is to go for volume and layer up a mix of foliage-heavy specimens."

8 Fill a terrarium

A glass terrarium filled with plants is a fun way to display greenery while keeping plants neatly enclosed. A vintage-style container will add character to a room, whereas a modern one will be right at home in a sleek, urban apartment. Good for containing any mess, easy to water and look after, terrariums are also a great way to introduce children to caring for plants, as they can create endless miniature worlds using small succulents or miniature houseplants.

9 Create a table centrepiece

Try potted plants as a dining-table centrepiece for a leafy alternative to cut flowers. Run a series of planters down the centre of the table for impact and dot tealights or tall candles among them for a romantic feel. For a special dinner party you could even place a tiny potted plant at each place setting as a take-home gift for your guests. I borrowed this idea from a friend, who gave each guest at her wedding a little succulent in a gold plant pot to take home – a much better alternative to the usual bag of sugared almonds.

"Houseplants are an easy way to connect your indoor and outdoor spaces and can create a pleasing visual link to any green space you have outside your home."

10 Blur the boundaries

Houseplants are an easy way to connect your indoor and outdoor spaces and can create a pleasing visual link to any green space you have outside your home. If you place a few floor-standing houseplants near to any outdoor access points, such as patio doors or balcony windows, this will immediately start to blur the boundaries between indoors and out. I tried this in my little guest bedroom, which had the potential to be a bit of a wasted space because it serves as a walk-through from the house to the back garden. I placed plants on both sides of the patio doors and this immediately gave the room a fresh lease of life and transformed it into a leafy extension of the garden.

And finally...

TAKE CARE

If you have children or pets at home, be aware that some houseplants can be poisonous, so do double-check before you introduce them to your living room. Children, especially babies and toddlers, have a habit of trying to eat anything and everything they can reach, so it is very important to ensure that any plants you place within potential reach of little fingers are nontoxic if ingested.

- Place plants out of reach of small hands and pets
- Cover pebbles or soil with mesh to prevent ingestion
- Choose nontoxic plants

How to Decorate with the Happiest Colour

If you had to choose the happiest colour, which shade would you go for? Sky blue, maybe? Ruby red? Or how about sunshine yellow? Colours can be very emotive and I bet you already use them, without realizing, to describe your emotions or state of mind. If you have ever described yourself as feeling "blue" or being "green with envy", for example, then you have already formed a link between colour and mood, but would it surprise you to learn that experts think they have discovered a universal "happiest colour"?

According to research undertaken by a team at the University of Manchester, when it comes to colours that make us feel happy, there is a clear winner that we can all agree on. And on the flipside, there is also an official "unhappy" colour.

Bring Me Sunshine

So, what are these happy and unhappy colours? Well, according to this research, the happiest colour is...yellow. And the unhappiest colour is...grey.

That sounds about right, doesn't it? The happiest colour brings to mind images of sunshine and warmth, while the unhappiest colour is redolent of rain clouds and chilly weather. But can it really be that clear-cut? And just how did researchers test this theory?

The discovery was the result of research undertaken by Professor Peter Whorwell and Dr Helen Carruthers, who carried out a study of people who were, and people who were not, anxious and depressed, to try to establish a link between colours and mood. They created a colour wheel using four shades of eight colours and grey, as well as black and white. They then asked everyone three questions: which colour represented their mood, which was their favourite and which they were drawn to.

The most popular "favourite colour", chosen by everyone, across the board, was blue. But, and this is where it gets interesting, when they were asked which colour they felt most "drawn to", both sets of participants mostly chose yellow. And when asked which colour represented their mood, yellow was most often associated with a "normal" mood and grey with an "anxious or depressed" mood. These findings led the researchers to conclude that yellow was most often linked with a happy mood and grey with an unhappy mood.

I asked Joa Studholme, International Colour Consultant for paint company Farrow & Ball, what she makes of this research. "I am a huge advocate of colour having mood-enriching properties," she says. "It's a powerful medium that has an effect at both a conscious and a subconscious level." But while she agrees that strong yellows "are certainly stimulating and engender a lively mood", she cautions against jumping right in and decorating with too much strong yellow, advising a less-is-more approach to avoid the risk of the shade looking too "garish".

With this in mind, over the next few pages I have pulled together some mood-boosting decorating tips, to show you how to decorate with the happiest colour in your own home.

Here Comes the Sun:
How to Decorate with Yellow

Small changes have a big impact with this sunny shade, so dip a toe in the water with one of these easy decorating updates and bring a little sunshine indoors.

Cast a warm light

A classic decorating trick to bring a soft glow to a room is to line the inside of a lampshade with a heat-resistant fabric in a warm shade of yellow or to choose one with a burnished gold interior, to instantly create warmth. Try this in rooms where you want to engender a soft, diffused atmosphere, such as a bedroom or a living room, or hang a yellow-lined pendant light low over a dining table to bathe your guests (and you) in a warm pool of flattering golden light.

Choosing yellow-toned lightbulbs is another instant and budget-friendly way to warm up the atmosphere of a room. If you have ever looked into the window of a bright, cheery living room from the outside on a dark evening, you will know the appeal of warm, yellow-hued light. Opening the front door on a dark winter's evening to be greeted by a glow of yellow light spilling out across the front step is a very welcoming sight to return home to.

"A glow of yellow light spilling out across the front step is a very welcoming sight to return home to."

Welcome guests

In an area that is just used as a transitional space, from outside to in, or from one room to the next, you can afford to be bold with colour. So try adding a splash of yellow to a hallway for a mood-enhancing lift every time you pass through. "A vibrant yellow hall is always welcoming," says Joa, so try bringing in a little sunshine with your décor choices. It doesn't have to be a big change, I have an egg-yolk-yellow vase near my front door that lifts my mood every time I see it, especially when it is filled with a cheery bunch of garden flowers. A painting with yellow tones or a bright yellow lampshade would have the same effect. Or, if you are feeling bold, dive right in and paint your walls a cheery buttercup yellow to add energy and zest to a hallway.

Mimic a sunny day

Joa suggests using yellow on windows "to create a sense of sunshine", and there are several ways to do this in your own home. Painting the inside trim of your windows is a great styling tip for mimicking the effect of warm sunshine and you don't have to choose a strong shade for this; even a soft wash of primrose yellow would have a cheering effect. Alternatively, you could hang a brightly coloured window blind or shade with yellow tones woven through the pattern to bring a sense of summer into your home all year round.

Show your sunny side

Yellow is a wonderful highlight colour and works well to draw attention to a key item of furniture. Treating a piece of vintage furniture to a coat of yellow paint is a great way to give it a new lease of life. To create a statement on a budget, try giving an old wooden chair a coat of buttercup-yellow paint and mixing it in with other chairs around a dining table. Or, for a more subtle flash of sunshine, update a country-style wooden dining table by painting the legs yellow to contrast with the warm grain of the wooden tabletop.

Walking on sunshine

Dark floors can be quickly and easily updated with a cheerful coloured rug, so if you want to add a burst of sunshine yellow underfoot, choose a brightly patterned rug and you will have happy feet every time you walk across it. Geometric patterns are a great partner for strong yellow shades and a cheery yellow-and-white patterned rug will instantly brighten up a gloomy hallway or add a fun touch to a children's playroom. Choose a hard-wearing or weatherproof rug and you can even add some yellow underfoot outdoors, too.

Scatter a little sunshine

Textiles are a quick and inexpensive way to change the look and feel of a room, so if you want to experiment with yellow but aren't sure about making a permanent commitment, test the waters with a buttercup-coloured throw or a scatter cushion in sunshine yellow. Mix in one or two yellow cushions with other cheery shades on a sofa to create a look you love, or try a soft wool throw across the foot of a bed to warm up a bedroom. Think about textures, too; velvet is a contemporary choice for accent cushions and one in mustard-yellow can look elegant and smart when placed against a grey or navy sofa.

Hang happy artwork

Changing your artwork is a great way to introduce colour to a room without the permanence of other design options. Don't be intimidated by choosing and buying art; the secret to deciding on any kind of décor for your home is just to ask yourself if you really love it – don't worry about what others will think or if it's a "good investment". If it cheers you each time you look at it, then it's money well spent, whether it's an original oil painting or a cheap and cheerful poster. If you are on a budget, then there are plenty of affordable ways to brighten up your walls. In my home office I have tacked up a display of postcards above the desk with yellow washi tape, and I update them whenever the mood takes me. You could also frame your favourite magazine covers, or paint picture frames a zesty citrus shade to bathe your photos in sunshine.

"The secret to deciding on any kind of décor for your home is just to ask yourself if you really love it – don't worry about what others will think."

Look to nature

First impressions count, so if you want to feel happy each time you open your front door, plant up colourful flowerpots with bold yellow flowers and group them directly outside the entrance to your home.

A climbing honeysuckle (*Lonicera*) or a rambling jasmine (*Jasminum*) would look wonderful around a front door if you have the space, or try a terracotta pot crammed with daffodils (*Narcissus*) in springtime. You could also plant sunflowers (*Helianthus*), primroses (*Primula*), tulips (*Tulipa*), roses (*Rosa*), magnolia (*Magnolia*) or any other yellow or gold-coloured flower that takes your fancy. Alternatively, you could choose (or paint) a sunny yellow plant pot and fill it with a mix of vibrantly coloured blooms to brighten up a porch or front step. Don't have any outside space? Try a hanging basket or window box instead.

When life gives you lemons

Lemon trees are surprisingly easy to look after, and the scent and sight of fresh, zingy lemons are mood-boosting tonics in themselves. I have a small lemon tree in a terracotta pot that I keep sheltered in the winter and move to a sunny spot as soon as the weather warms up. I bought it after a trip to the Amalfi coast in Italy, where lemon trees line the streets and their fresh, summery scent perfumes the air. Small citrus trees can have a long fruiting season if you look after them carefully and I can't recommend them enough – the joy you will get from seeing each new yellow fruit peeking out from underneath the waxy green leaves is a great reward for your efforts. As well as these little droplets of yellow treasure, my tree also provides the prettiest snow white blossom, the scent of which is like bottled sunshine and instantly transports me back to the sparkling seas and sunny beaches of Capri.

Create Your Own Sunshine:
How to Make Yellow Work Whatever Your Style

There is a yellow out there for everyone and the tone you choose can have a huge impact on the mood you subsequently create. "Rooms can be made to feel more formal or relaxed with the use of colour," agrees Joa, "colder colours being more formal and warmer colours more relaxed. Small rooms can become flamboyant with strong colour and large rooms become airy by lack of colour."

Make it traditional

If bright citrus isn't the shade for you, you can introduce mellower, warmer tones of buttercup and caramel, and mix them in with buttery neutrals for a softer look in a traditional-style interior. These quieter tones would sit more comfortably with dark wood furniture and classic décor, and, in this setting, soft yellow can almost be used in the same way as a neutral. Layer up different tones to add interest, bring in plenty of texture and contrast it with crisp white for an elegant feel.

Take it to the country

Yellow can also look surprisingly at home in a country-style interior. The key is to bring in elements of rich, egg-yolk yellow and contrast them with pretty, bright florals and/or soft stripes, and keep the finish matt for a casual look. A country-style dresser, for example, would look wonderful painted a rich, warm yellow and filled with a selection of mismatched crockery, cheerful table linens and a container of garden flowers.

Be bright and beautiful

Yellow is a powerful shade, so it can have a real impact in a contemporary home. Add a playful touch by introducing a flash of zesty colour where it is going to be least expected, such as the lining of a curtain or around a doorframe. Painting the inside edge of a door is another way to defy convention and reveal a small sliver of sunshine each time you open it. Just be sure to use this accent colour sparingly, to highlight small details, add drama or introduce an element of fun.

Find Your Own Happy

While yellow seems to be the winner for the happiest colour, according to the experiment carried out by Professer Whorwell and Dr Carruthers, there were several other colours on the wheel that had positive connotations, and the truth is that everyone will see colour differently. While you might want to use yellow in some rooms to create an uplifting mood, you will also want to create different moods in other areas of the home. "Most people want to create either a sense of calm or a feeling of intimacy," agrees Joa. "The magic of colour is that you can do this with ease."

So if yellow isn't the shade for you, or if you want to use colour to create different moods in different areas of your home, take a look at the colour chart below and discover your own happy shades.

1 **Pick your mood**
Look at the colour chart and write down how each colour makes you feel: happy, sad, calm or energized.

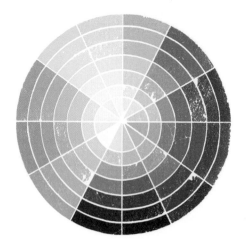

2 **List your rooms**
Now write down how you want to feel in each room of your home: living room, kitchen, bedroom, bathroom, office and children's room.

3 **You've got a match!**
Now match up your moods and rooms. For example, if you decided that soft blue was the colour that made you feel the most relaxed and calm, and you also identified that you want your bedroom to make you feel this way, then you've got a match. Get everyone in your home to do the same and you will start to build up a colour-mood map that you can use to decorate your home.

Things You Need to Know Before You Start Decorating

I asked Joa for her colour decorating tips to help you get started with adding colour to your rooms. "The joy of decorating with colour is that there are no rules!" says Joa. "It is the best way to express one's individuality. However, I always advise people to think about the following three things before they start."

1 Consider the light in the room
"Embrace it, don't fight it, which often means painting darker spaces in stronger, darker colours and light spaces in light, airy colours."

2 Think about more than just the colour on the walls
"You need to make choices about the woodwork, ceiling and any bits of joinery or painted furniture, too. They are all like small ingredients in a recipe, which need to be perfectly balanced within the room."

3 Always choose colours that you feel comfortable with
"You don't need to use colours that are historically correct for your architecture and you certainly don't have to use grey just because everyone else is!"

And finally...

While grey didn't win any prizes in the happy colour contest, this versatile shade still has a lot to recommend it and it has had a huge surge in popularity recently. So I asked Joa to offer some tips on using grey to create a good mood in the home.

"Grey has been, without doubt, the most fashionable colour to use in the home for the past five years and it certainly does not create an unhappy atmosphere. However, you need to take care to use warmer greys, especially in north light (in the northern hemisphere) when cold greys can feel too gritty and industrial for most homes. Lighter grey on the walls with a slightly darker grey on the woodwork will create a space that remains light and airy but has a feeling of sophistication."

3

Tidy Your Way to Happiness

Can a tidy home make you healthier and happier? According to research, yes, it can. Darby E. Saxbe and Rena Repetti, researchers at UCLA, discovered that women who described their living spaces as "cluttered" or full of "unfinished projects" were more likely to be depressed and fatigued than women who described their homes as "restful" and "restorative". It sounds obvious, doesn't it? A tidy home makes us happy and a messy one makes us unhappy. Worryingly, these researchers also found that women with a cluttered home produced higher levels of the stress hormone cortisol. But can you reverse this trend and clean your way to happiness and health? Absolutely! According to a study in the *British Journal of Sports Medicine* (*BJSM*), cleaning your home vigorously for 20 minutes nonstop once a week can improve levels of anxiety, distress or depression. So if you want to grab some of those health benefits for yourself, it's time to wave goodbye to stressful clutter and say hello to a tidy, streamlined home. This chapter will show you how.

Six Daily Habits of Tidy People

If you like the idea of a tidy home but clutter seems to just build up at every turn, don't worry, you are not alone. But there is a way to fake it until you make it. Here are six habits to borrow from tidy people (I borrowed them from my sister).

 Just do it
Waiting for the perfect moment to declutter your home? Here's the secret: that moment is now. Tidy people like my sister don't leave jobs until later, they pick up clutter as soon as they see it, they wash their dishes when they have finished eating and they make the bed as soon as they hop out of it. Yes, those people really do exist, and yes, you can become one too, with a little practice.

  Make a list
If chores seem unsurmountable, break them down into bite-sized chunks and work through them methodically. Messy people see clutter as an unscalable mountain. Tidy people see it as a series of gentle hill walks.

 Find a place for everything
Here's the secret: tidy people don't have piles of assorted items all over their home because *they have a dedicated space for everything.* That's literally it. If I finish reading a magazine at my sister's house, I'll leave it on the table and minutes later it's whisked away into the magazine rack; if I put my phone on the kitchen counter, it's moved to the charging dock in the hallway. I've implemented a version of this (admittedly, a more relaxed version) in my own home and it really does work.

4 Tidy as you go

Cooking a meal? Tidy people will clear up as they go, rather than leave a pile of pots and pans and dirty chopping boards for later. The same applies to a craft or DIY project; if you get out a stack of art materials or a pot of paint and a paintbrush, put them away as soon as you have finished with them, rather than leaving a mess to deal with later. Think of it as short-term pain, long-term gain. The happiness of finishing a meal and knowing there is no washing-up to be done is not to be underestimated.

5 Make your bed

Tidy people know that just pulling the bedding up and plumping the pillows immediately after getting out of bed makes the bedroom look instantly tidy and organized and starts your day off on the right foot. I've begun doing it and it's incredibly good for giving you a smug little glow first thing in the morning. Plus it only takes 30 seconds, so everyone has time for that. Do it.

6 Edit down

Do you need two of those? Really? Tidy people will ruthlessly edit down the items in their home on a regular basis. They don't need to have a huge declutter because they don't let items build up in the first place. Cast a similarly critical eye over your home and start to filter out unnecessary items on a daily basis. Cupboard full of kitchen appliances you only used once? Sell or donate them. Old coats cluttering up your hall cupboard? Donate them to a charity and claim back your storage space.

Five Things to Get Rid Of Today

 Clothes that don't fit or flatter
Trust me, if you haven't worn an item of clothing in the past year, you are not likely to wear it in the next 12 months. Clothes need to make you feel amazing, so anything that doesn't make you feel great, flatter your figure or work hard for its keep needs to go. A commonly suggested tip for this is to turn all your clothes hangers to face away from you in your wardrobe, then as you wear something, turn the hanger back to face you. Any hangers that haven't been turned around over the course of a year indicate that the item needs to go. It works.

 Old college notes or memorabilia
Yes, you put a lot of work into your university degree, but what are you keeping all your old research notes for? Are you planning to review them all one day? Or perhaps you might invite all your friends and family over one evening and read sections aloud to them? If the honest answer is no (and I hope it is), then it's time to let them go. The same goes for old tickets, catalogues or brochures that you kept for sentimental value. Allow yourself to keep a few items that really mean a lot to you and store them neatly in a box, then recycle everything else.

3 Old phones, chargers and tech items

Keeping tech "just in case" is a surefire way to acquire a drawer full of items you won't use. Don't do it. Take any old phones, tablets or computers to recycling centres or trade them in for money off your next purchase.

4 Old kitchen gadgets

If it's broken, gathering dust or hasn't been used for the past two years, it's time to recycle or donate it. Yes, that means the bread maker, the ice-cream maker and the mountains of old plastic boxes. Once you've cut the apron strings and got rid of all those items you've been hoarding "just in case", you will instantly free up valuable kitchen cupboard space.

5 Old paperwork

As a guide, keep one year's worth of bills and paperwork and seven years' worth of tax records, then shred the rest, but do check with your tax advisor to find out exactly what you need to keep. If you work from home you may need to keep several years' worth of paperwork for tax reasons.

NOTE
Old electrical items need to be disposed of properly, usually at a recycling centre.

Five Clutter Hotspots...

...and How to Banish Them

Bedside tables

In theory, your bedside table would accommodate just a thought-provoking novel, an elegant reading lamp and a glass for water; in reality, it's probably piled up with an awful lot more than that. Because bedrooms have limited worksurfaces, bedside tables are magnets for clutter; so here's how to impose a sense of order and calm.

Edit ruthlessly

Visual clutter, reminding you of jobs you need to do, is really unhelpful when you are trying to drift off to sleep. So ask yourself what you actually need by your bed and edit accordingly. I tried this in my own bedroom and ended up removing seven unread books, two magazines, three pairs of earrings, two pairs of sunglasses, several hairbands and a hairbrush. The only items I kept were a reading lamp, one book and a tray for my jewellery. If you find your bedside table magically accumulates clutter, like mine did, try a similar edit and be ruthless.

Create a "pocket tray"

Think about your bedtime routine. If you tend to remove your jewellery or empty your pockets before you climb into bed, get a tray or storage box to corral all of these small items and keep them tidy. Loose change, cufflinks, earrings and keys are all common clutter culprits, so allocate them a box and sweep them into it every evening. This can be one of the items you allow yourself to keep on your bedside table.

Choose a table with storage

With the best will in the world, clutter will accumulate, so pre-empt it by choosing a bedside table with storage drawers or baskets, then do a clean sweep every night and put anything non-essential into a drawer or stash it in a basket and tuck it away under the table.

Bathroom worktops

Perfume bottles, toothpaste tubes, empty shampoo bottles...clutter can build up at a mystifyingly rapid rate in a bathroom when several members of the family are using it to get ready first thing in the morning. These quick tips will help to restore order.

Divide and conquer

Impose order by allocating each member of the family their own drawer or container and keeping only a few items out on the countertop. If you don't have enough storage space for everyone to have a drawer, colourful boxes or wicker baskets are good alternatives. Sweep all non-essential items into these containers after use and pop the lid on to regain some order. A colourful box for corralling children's bath toys is also a good idea if you want to limit the bath-time chaos and avoid stepping on a hard plastic toy with bare feet (you'll only do it once!).

Group essentials

For those items that are used everyday and need to be kept out on the countertop, such as hand wash, hand lotion and toothbrushes, group them all together on a tray and keep them close to the sink to avoid splashing water all over the countertop when you

reach for them. Choose beautiful bottles or containers that you will be happy to look at every day, too; I decant my liquid hand soap into a glass soap dispenser because I'd rather look at that than a plastic bottle, but I realize that might be a step too far for some people.

Tidy towels

Large storage boxes are good for keeping clean towels neatly ordered, and plenty of wall hooks will ensure wet towels don't end up on the floor after a shower. Colour-coded towels are useful if you have lots of people using a bathroom – and culprits can be easily identified when damp towels are left on the floor. A simple coloured tab or marker-pen dot on the label are ways to allocate towels if they are all the same colour. If you are really organized, why not take a leaf out of my sister's book and embroider the name of each family member onto their own set of towels? Instant identification!

That kitchen drawer

You know the one – the drawer that's stuffed with takeout menus, batteries, scissors, pens, paperclips, old receipts and who knows what else. We all have one of these offenders and, actually, we all need one; where else would you file all those random items that don't belong anywhere else? But the key to keeping on top of it all is to regularly dive in and sort through it.

Take stock

Clear everything out of the drawer and group like with like. Roll up lengths of string neatly together, stack menus in a pile and sort through all those single batteries to see which are charged and which need to be recycled. If there is a more logical place to store something, find it a new home. If there really isn't anywhere else for it to live, then it can go back in the drawer. But be strict.

Buy a dividing tray

Find a tray or dividing system for the drawer (a cutlery tray is good for this) and allocate a space for each of the different groups of items. Now fill it up section by section. Place all of the essential items that you need to access daily (pens, scissors, string) at the front and move those that are used less often (batteries, menus) to the back.

Banish layers

The tipping point for a messy drawer is usually when several items get layered up on top of each other, because as soon as you start having to sift around to find what you need, looking under papers and behind rolls of string, the whole thing quickly unravels. So be strict with yourself and don't put anything on top of your newly ordered storage system. If it doesn't fit into a compartment, then it doesn't go in the drawer.

The hallway floor

Your hallway will need to work extra hard to stay tidy with the amount of daily traffic it has to deal with and the number of items that need to be accessed every day. If you find yourself tripping over shoes, umbrellas or children's toys the second you walk through the door, it could be time for a blitz. Here's how to transform your hallway from cluttered to calm.

Storage, storage, storage

I am obsessed with storage and don't think you can ever have too much. Hallway storage, in particular, can be really appealing; wall hooks, post trays, umbrella stands and storage benches can totally transform a cluttered hallway and provide a great opportunity to stamp your personality on your home.

Floor space is usually limited, so start with the walls. Peg rails are great for a country-style hall and can be run right along the length of your hallway for maximum coat storage, or choose brightly coloured hooks for a cheery welcome in a contemporary space. Named hooks are good for allocating each member of the family a designated space to hang their coat, and high shelves are good for stashing away items that aren't needed every day.

Be seasonal

In the height of summer do you need to have wet-weather gear cluttering up the hallway? And, equally, do you need to take up valuable storage space with sandals and beach bags in the winter? Have a seasonal review of your hallway cupboards and remove any items that aren't required. Store them somewhere else, such as under a guest bed or in the attic, until they are needed again, then swap them over for the new season's items.

Squeeze in a slim table

Somewhere for keys, mail and your phone is essential in a hallway, if you want to keep these things in one place and avoid dropping them on various tables around the house instead. If you have enough space to squeeze in a slim console table, it will definitely pull its weight. The secret to blissful order is to place a few trays or dishes on top and allocate one for each item that you tend to put down when you walk through the door.

Kitchen worktops

The kitchen is another hard-working space that gets a lot of daily traffic, and kitchen worktops in particular can accumulate clutter at an alarming speed. I find that stray pieces of paperwork, such as unpaid bills and receipts, mysteriously migrate to my kitchen worktop – I have no idea how – along with a motley selection of items "on their way to somewhere else". Here are a few ways to keep surfaces clean-swept and tidy.

Have an in-tray

If letters, bills and homework books tend to migrate to your kitchen worktop, set up a box or tray to keep them tidy and together. A slim tray is better, as a large box will only encourage paperwork to build up, making the problem worse. If you use it as an active in-tray, to be sorted through daily, it will keep everything in one place and prevent individual letters and bills from drifting across the worktop.

Maximize wall storage

Clutter attracts more clutter, so clearing your worktops of anything that is non-essential will allow you a clean slate from which to start. Many items that clutter up kitchen worktops can usually be hung on the wall with a little creative thought. Try hanging utensils from a bar or series of hooks, store spices and herbs on a wall-mounted rack and place vegetables in wall-hung wire containers.

Limit food containers on worktops

It's nice to have a few everyday essentials out on the worktop, such as a bowl of fruit, but when food containers start to take over the worktop it's time to be ruthless. Store most food items in cupboards or out of sight and just display one or two items that you like to see every day.

4

Unlock the Secret to a Good Night's Sleep

When was the last time you had a really good night's sleep? I mean the kind of deep, refreshing sleep that enables you to spring out of bed the next morning, full of optimism and energy for the day ahead? If you can't remember the last occasion, then it could be time to overhaul your sleeping habits and start to take your rest time seriously, because a good sleep routine is one of the most crucial elements to get right if you want to boost your health, wellbeing and happiness levels at home.

Can a Good Night's Sleep Make Us Happier?

No one doubts the mood-boosting magic of a good night's sleep, but I wanted to find out just why so many of us struggle to get enough of it and what happens to our bodies when we don't hit our nightly quota. I set out to discover if and how we can reverse negative sleep patterns, to unearth the simple and easy steps we can all take to improve our sleep at home and how to attain that magical eight hours of refreshing slumber each and every night.

I quizzed Lisa Artis, spokesperson for The Sleep Council, about all things relaxing. "Just one bad night's sleep affects our mood, concentration and alertness," says Lisa, "while long-term sleep deprivation has far more serious consequences: it's been linked to a number of serious health problems, such as high blood pressure, heart disease, diabetes and stroke." But before you panic your way to another sleepless night, Lisa is also a huge advocate of the positive impact of a good night's sleep on health and happiness levels, and she has some practical advice about how we can all reset our bad habits.

So if we overhaul our sleeping habits and routines, can this make us happier? "It certainly can!" says Lisa. "As with proper nutrition and exercise, sleep fulfils a vital role in keeping us healthy and happy. We need a good night's sleep to ensure we're feeling fit, thinking sharply and generally have the appetite and enthusiasm to make the most of everyday living."

> *"A good sleep routine is one of the most crucial elements to get right if you want to boost your health, wellbeing and happiness levels at home."*

The Action Plan

The best place to start when resetting your sleep routines and undoing bad sleep habits is, naturally, your bedroom. There are a few common mistakes that we are all guilty of – reading your phone in bed, anyone? – so I asked Lisa what the top offenders are when it comes to disturbed sleep. On the following pages I will show you quick and easy ways to fix these.

Four things at home that may be ruining your sleep...

1 **Daylight**
Getting the light levels right in your bedroom can have a big impact on sleep – too much light can hamper your ability to get your nightly ZZZs. "A dark room is most conducive to sleep, as light tells your body it's time to wake up," explains Lisa. "In darkness, your body releases a hormone called melatonin that relaxes your body, helping you to drift off." (See also page 95.)

2 **Heat**
Struggle to drift off to sleep in the summer months? If your bedroom is too hot, it could be preventing you from getting good-quality sleep. "Ideally, bedrooms should be around 16–18°C (60–65°F)," says Lisa. "Your body temperature needs to lower slightly before you go to sleep, which is why it's difficult to drop off when you're too hot."

3 **Tech**
Do you go to bed at a sensible hour, full of good intentions to get an early night, only to then spend an hour aimlessly scrolling through your social media accounts, watching videos of cats and online shopping? If so, you are not alone, but it could be time to cut the habit. "All this nonstop stimulation causes havoc when we're trying to fall asleep," says Lisa. "Switch off your tech at least an hour before bedtime, and that includes your phone."

4 **Colours**
What colour is your bedroom? If it is a strong or bright shade, it could be time to get out the paint and paintbrush. "Strong colours can stimulate your energy, resulting in poor sleep," warns Lisa. "Conversely, pastels and calming shades promote a more relaxing environment."

...and How to Fix Them

Now we know what is preventing us from falling asleep, but what is the answer? The following steps will help you to create a snug, cosy and cool bedroom that will allow you to drift effortlessly into a peaceful night's sleep. No sheep counting required.

Block the light

Make sure your curtains are long enough

Drapes that stop too short, or at windowsill height, will usually still let in slivers of light around the edges, so if you can, invest in long ones that sweep right down to the floor to help block any light from sneaking into the room. I love the luxurious effect of curtains gently pooling onto the floor, especially when they are made of linen or lightweight fabrics, so I made sure that the curtains in my bedroom were just a bit longer than the drop from curtain rail to floor to allow for this. If this isn't your thing – and it does divide opinion – then just ensure that your drapes lightly brush the floor instead. The key is to avoid them hovering shy of the carpet because, as well as allowing light to sneak in, this also has the unfortunate effect of making them look like a pair of trousers that are too short.

Double up

If you want to really lightproof your room, you will need to layer up your window treatments. I have installed a light-coloured blackout blind to sit within the window frame of my bedroom window, as well as heavy linen curtains in front, and the two of these combined ensure the room is dark, cocooning and restful when it needs to be. Double window treatments are also a great way to play with pattern in a bedroom; a patterned blind hung behind plain curtains will add a shot of colour and interest during the day and can be tucked out of sight behind restful curtains at night.

Use blackout fabric

Blackout fabric is your secret weapon in the fight against daylight and is particularly invaluable in a child's bedroom if you need to darken the space for midday naps or early bedtimes. Drapes can be backed or interlined with blackout fabric for really good light protection, and blinds can be made in blackout fabric, too. If you double up blackout blinds and blackout curtains, you really will create a hibernation-worthy den.

Play it cool
Go natural

To keep your body temperature at a comfortable level during the night, choose cotton or linen sheets over man-made materials; the same goes for anything you wear in bed. Natural materials will allow your skin to breathe and will help to wick away moisture and regulate your temperature throughout the night. Investing in a summer/winter duvet is a good option for temperature regulation, too; these are usually made of two lightweight duvets that can be used individually in the summer months and then fastened together to create a heavyweight layer for winter hibernation.

Create a cool breeze

Even with the right bedding, trying to get to sleep on hot summer nights can be a struggle if your room isn't properly ventilated, so it is important to try to keep your bedroom as cool as possible during the day. In hot weather, keep the windows open and the curtains drawn during the day to keep the temperature low and use a fan if you need to bring the temperature down further before sleep. Last summer, during an unseasonably hot heatwave, when it seemed that the entire country was struggling to sleep, a friend shared a great tip with me for creating instant (and cheap) air-conditioning: place a bowl of iced water in front of a tabletop fan, angled so that the air from

the fan skims across the ice, and you get a deliciously cool stream of "iced air". It really does work and it's a great trick to try on those days when the air is stiflingly hot.

Make a cold-water bottle

Hot-water bottles are usually associated with chilly evenings and brisk winter nights, for obvious reasons, but on a very warm summer's night, try filling your hot-water bottle with cold water and pop it in the freezer for a few hours to create an iced-water bottle. Pop it under the covers an hour or so before bedtime so that when you climb into bed it will be deliciously cool.

> *"An hour spent browsing social media accounts on your phone before bed could tell your mind that you are not ready for sleep, while your exhausted body is trying to tell you that you are."*

Turn off tech

Minimize blue light

Are you feeling "tired but wired?" An overload of blue light from digital devices at night-time can play havoc with your sleep patterns, as it interferes with the body's production of melatonin, which can lead to the effect of being physically tired but mentally alert. For example, an hour spent browsing social media accounts on your phone before bed could tell your mind that you are not ready for sleep, while your exhausted body is trying to tell you that you are. To get back on track, try limiting your use of phones and tablets before bed or, if you really can't face doing that, switch the screen to night-time mode to reduce the levels of blue light (see page 154).

Banish LED displays

Bright LED displays on alarm clocks can be a distracting light source when you are trying to drift off, plus having a visual reminder of the time when you are desperately trying to get to sleep is never helpful. Choose an analogue clock instead, or one without a backlit display, to get rid of any unnecessary light in the bedroom.

Switch off the TV

TVs in bedrooms are a tricky topic. Many people have them and, yes, they are convenient for watching a movie before you go to sleep, but they can dominate the one room that is supposed to be a calm and peaceful retreat from the rest of your home. Add to this the fact that they can also seriously hamper our ability to sleep and I am ready to ban them from the bedroom. But if you aren't ready to banish your bedroom TV, then at least make sure you switch it off well before you try to go to sleep, as the flickering screen can disrupt the production of the sleep hormone melatonin.

Pick relaxing colours
Choose relaxing shades

Soothing colours are essential in a bedroom, where the aim is to create a peaceful environment to help you to unwind from the day and transition into sleep. Soft tones are better than bright, energizing colours but colour is very subjective, so the key is just to choose a shade that you identify as soothing and calming (see page 34). Consider soft shades of blue, light neutrals or gentle pastel tones.

Plump for natural-toned bed linen

Your bed linen will make up a considerable proportion of the colour palette in your bedroom, so choose it wisely. A plain white or light-toned duvet or comforter cover is much more relaxing to look at than a busy, patterned one, which is visually stimulating and not conducive to winding down. If you do want to bring in a colour, layer up a patterned throw or bedspread on top of a plain cover.

Consider artwork

Soothing scenes or abstract canvases can work better in a bedroom than busy pictures or brightly coloured artwork, which can be too energizing. Pick patterns or scenes that make you feel rested and calm or choose a print with a calming mantra.

Elevate Your Evening Ritual:
Four Nightly Rituals to Help You Unwind

Now you have set your bedroom up for optimum sleep, it is time to think about how you can carve out some time each night to mentally and physically unwind and move yourself into a more relaxed frame of mind before bed. Here are some evening relaxation routines that you can adopt to ensure you are in the right state of mind when your head hits the pillow.

Write your worries down

I am really bad at allowing lots of small worries to build up into one large, looming cloud of anxiety, and these worry clouds tend to gather just when I need to drift off to sleep. If you also find yourself wide awake at 2am with an undefinable sense of anxiety, it can really help to write everything down and try to get some perspective on exactly what is worrying you. Before you go to bed, make a note of everything that is troubling you, from the big concerns to the tiny ones, then try to write an action point next to each item. For example, are you worried about a presentation you have to do at work? Write down the worry and then add a note to ask a colleague to help you with a run-through in the morning, for example. It won't instantly banish all your concerns, but it will turn them into more manageable items and might allow your brain a little bit of breathing space.

② Take a warm (not hot) bath

Any routine or habit that allows you to transition from a busy day to a more relaxed state of mind before bedtime is a good thing. Taking a bath just before bed can really help you to switch into sleep mode and if you add a relaxing scent into the mix, such as lavender bath oil, you get extra points. But do make sure the bath water is warm, as opposed to piping hot, and avoid really strong scents because both of these things are actually counterintuitive to sleep.

3. Plan your next day in advance

I am always in a rush in the mornings. No matter how much I would like to be calm and organized, there always seems to be a sense of urgency – some might say drama – to my mornings. So to be kind to my future self, I have started planning the next morning before I go to bed. I think about where I need to be the next day, decide what I am going to wear and put my bag ready by the front door to try to mitigate any last-minute drama. I spend extra time doing this if I know I have a particularly busy day ahead or an important event coming up, because otherwise I will lie awake worrying about it and waste precious sleep time. So if you find that you are getting anxious about the next day, or if, like me, you are just not a morning person, try to spend a few minutes before you get into bed mentally running through the day ahead and prepping in any way you can. That allows you to go to bed with an easy mind and, dare I say it, a touch of smugness, too.

4. Set a "bedtime"

If you have children, you will know the importance of routines, especially when it comes to nap times and bedtimes. Treat your own sleep in the same way and try to go to bed and wake up at around the same time each day to establish a sleep routine. I get up for work every day at 7am, so I aim to be in bed by 11pm and I try to treat my weekends the same way. Admittedly, this can be difficult if you have had a busy week and want to treat yourself to a lie-in at the weekend, so don't be too hard on yourself if you don't get up at precisely the same time every day, but if you can stick to roughly the same bedtime routine, regardless of weekdays or weekends, it will really help you to regulate your sleep.

And Finally...

How to Find Your Dream Sleep Partner

If you've followed all the steps in this chapter so far, you've now optimized your bedroom design, you've chosen soothing colours, written down all your worries and put technology firmly in its place. But there's still one, very crucial element to get right. Your bed. Choosing the right bed and mattress is crucial in the quest for a peaceful, relaxed slumber, so I asked The Sleep Council to shed some light on how to choose the perfect bed. They suggest asking yourself the following questions about your mattress and the quality of your sleep.

Do you need a new bed?

If the answer is yes to any of the following questions, it is time to find yourself a new bed.

☐ Have you had your mattress for more than seven years?

☐ Do you wake up with stiffness and/or aches and pains?

☐ Are you sleeping worse than you did a year ago?

☐ Have you had a better night's sleep in a bed other than yours?

☐ Does your mattress show signs of visible wear and tear (it sags, is lumpy and so on)?

TOP TIP

Set aside enough time to do the job properly. Don't shop when you are tired or rushed – you run the risk that all the beds will feel wonderful.

What size?

If you share your bed, The Sleep Council recommend that you should both be able to lie side by side with your arms behind your head and your elbows out, without touching. They also suggest that your bed is 10–15cm (4–6in) longer than the tallest partner.

Take the test

A good way to check if the bed you are lying on is too soft, too hard or just right is to lie on your back and slide your hand under the hollow of your back. If it slides in too easily, the bed may be too hard for you (leading to pressure on your hips and shoulders). If it is a struggle to slide your hand in, then the bed is probably too soft. If you can move your hand with just a little resistance, the bed may be just right for you.

Sleep tight!

5

Discover the Happiest Scents

Scent can be an intensely individual thing and fragrances are often tightly woven with memories. If you have ever experienced a rush of nostalgia when a particular perfume catches you unawares, you will know how deeply personal our sense of smell can be. On the other hand, we can more or less agree that there are a few universally accepted "good" and "bad" smells. Name me one person who dislikes the delicate perfume of a rose in bloom on a sunny day, for example.

But while we may agree on the power of scent to boost our mood, how many of us actively consider it when we create our home environment? For such a powerful sense, smell is often largely overlooked as part of an interior scheme. You might light the odd scented candle or buy a bunch of flowers now and again, but would you like to know how to use scent to shape and improve your mood at home? If the answer is yes, read on.

Can Scent Boost Our Wellbeing?

I set out to discover if there were universally accepted scents that could lower stress, increase happiness and promote relaxation at home, and I started my research by talking to Roja Dove, master perfumer and a board director of The Fragrance Foundation. "Fragrance is one of the best things you can buy to make you feel good," he told me, "as each ingredient works on our subconscious, releasing hormones which, among other things, give us energy, lift our mood or enhance sensations of pleasure."

Roja agrees that the link to memory is integral to the power that scent has on our mood. "A perfume brings back moments in our lives in vivid, glorious technicolour," he says. "It has the ability to bring a smile to our lips, or tears to our eyes; it can both repel us and attract us." So can we add to our memories and create new scent associations through the way we fragrance our homes? Roja thinks we can. "Our responses to scent are learned," he says, "each one locked away with a memory of association about whatever was happening to us at the time."

So could scent carry the key to happiness at home? Nicola Elliott, founder and creative director of wellness brand Neom Organics, thinks so. "Essential oils can be a natural antidote to the frenetic pace of life," she says, "and fragrance is so important for creating an atmosphere and emotion in the home."

"Fragrance is one of the best things you can buy to make you feel good."

The "happiest" scents

I asked Nicola and Roja to share their secrets for improving sleep quality, boosting mood and increasing energy at home, as well as attaining that all-important "happiness" factor.

How to improve sleep

"There are countless studies that prove the relaxing qualities of lavender," says Nicola, and it is commonly used to encourage a good night's sleep, in both dried form and as an essential oil. Lavender is very easy to grow yourself, so if you have a balcony or terrace, try growing a small plant in a container (see page 74). "Jasmine is another deeply relaxing oil, known for its soothing properties," says Nicola. Roja also names lavender, chamomile, bergamot, jasmine, rose and sandalwood as essential oils that all have soothing, calming qualities "to help encourage sleep and relaxation".

How to boost energy

"Grapefruit, sparkling lemon and rosemary are all excellent scents to help refresh and energize," says Nicola. "Citrus notes have been used for centuries to revive, uplift, inject life and boost vitality," agrees Roja. "Think about the effect of someone peeling an orange in a stuffy train carriage – it

instantly recharges the stale, stagnant air. Citrus notes are mainly used in the top notes of a fragrance, which means – like that orange – the burst of energy is short-lived. You have to spritz little and often to keep your boost going." It is actually possible to grow citrus fruit in cooler climates, if you keep them sheltered and protected during winter. The small lemon tree I have at home always boosts my mood, thanks to both the vibrant colour of its fruit (see page 31) and the incredible scent of its blossom in spring.

How to increase happiness

"Whatever your version of happiness is, we believe it starts with a positive state of mind," says Nicola. "Happiness means different things to different people, but you can definitely use essential oils to lift your spirits and inspire a little optimism." She suggests mimosa, white neroli and lemon, to boost the mood, as well as energizing wild mint and uplifting mandarin, "to help calm the body while improving circulation and boosting immunity". "Sandalwood has been proven in scientific trials to increase positive feelings," adds Roja, "and vanilla is a psychogenic aphrodisiac which enhances positive sensations."

How to Choose the Right Scent for Each Room

Still not sure which scent you need? I asked Roja if there were certain scents that suited different rooms in the home. "Because of our individual interior styles, there are no hard-and-fast rules as to what scents work in what spaces," he admits, "though as a generalization, cosseting scents like amber and vanilla work wonderfully to create a cosy atmosphere for an evening in the living room, while gourmand scents, such as herbs, spices and fruits, help keep a kitchen smelling fresh and full of flavour. Anything fresh works well in the bathroom, but overall you can never go wrong with the uplifting aroma of citrus notes in any room."

Create happy memories

"When we discover a scent we truly love, it will have ingredients within it that have positive, feel-good associations," says Roja. "The scent itself then becomes an odour that also has positive associations and makes us feel safe, secure, happy and well."

"Your body knows best what your mind needs most."

Trust your instincts

"Most of all, listen to yourself," says Nicola, and trust your own instincts. "Choose scents that make you feel calm and content; your body knows best what your mind needs most".

A rose by any other name...

Could a floral scent be a quick shortcut to happiness? Quite possibly, according to research led by Jeannette Haviland-Jones, of Rutgers University, New Jersey. As reported in LiveScience.com, the researchers ran an experiment in which they perfumed a room with either a floral smell, a classic fragrance like Chanel No 5 or Johnson's Baby Powder, or nonscented air. They then asked 59 college students to write about three life events. The essays were then coded for the number of positive and negative words used. Participants in the florally scented room used about three times as many happiness-related words in their writings. Time to invest in a bunch of fresh flowers, perhaps?

Banish the Bad

Before you start adding beautiful scents to your home, though, you will need to banish any bad odours that might be lingering. Here's how to scrub your home slate clean.

Scrub out your refrigerator

Out-of-date food and spilled liquids can quickly create an unpleasant odour in a refrigerator that can be hard to shift. Keeping the contents of your refrigerator neatly labelled and organized is a good way to keep on top of what you have and to avoid the unpleasant surprise of discovering a rotten tomato liquefying, forgotten, on a shelf. It is also a good idea to give your refrigerator a good scrub clean every couple of months, removing all the shelves and giving them a hot soak in the sink while you wipe down the inside of the door and the walls.

Put any cleaning cloths through a hot wash

Dishcloths, scrubbing brushes and floor mops can soak up all kinds of unpleasant aromas, so keep on top of any bacteria build-up by putting them through a regular hot-wash cycle and replace them frequently to keep them in tiptop condition.

Clean any pet bedding

If you are a pet owner, you will know how quickly a pet smell can permeate soft furnishings, so keeping on top of cleaning out litter trays and freshening up pet beds will probably be second nature to you. Keeping a small hand-held vacuum cleaner close by, to banish dog or cat hairs, is a good idea, as well as regularly washing your pet's bedding and any cloth toys on a hot cycle.

Refresh flower water

If you have ever been away for a few days and left a vase of flowers in a window, you will know how unpleasant the odour can be on your return, but this can build up after just a couple of days, too. Flower stems can decay quickly if left in direct sunlight and the water can turn slimy and stale. Keep your vases regularly topped up with fresh water and try adding a (tiny) drop of bleach to kill off any bacteria (see page 79). And if you are going away for a few days, remember to empty your cut flowers onto the compost heap before you leave.

Clean your washing machine

If you don't regularly clean out your washing machine, you might notice that your clothes are not coming out as fresh as they should be. It is simple to fix, though; just remove the detergent tray once a week and scrub it clean to prevent any soap build-up, and add a cleaning agent to an empty hot wash once a month to get rid of any bacteria and leave it sparklingly clean. You will also need to wipe down the rubber seal around the door after every couple of washes because stale water can accumulate there.

Unblock sinks and drains

Cleaning out sink and bathtub drains might not be the most glamorous job in the world, but you will need to tackle it in order to keep your home smelling fresh. Regularly clear out any drain traps and every month flush them through with a cleaning agent and hot water to check for blockages.

Ways to Fragrance Your Home

Now you have chosen the fragrance you want to bring into your home, here are a few ways to do so.

 Oil burner
An oil burner consists of a ceramic dish, into which you place a little water with a few drops of essential oil, over a tealight. When the tealight is lit, it warms up the oil and releases the aroma into the room. Good for creating a soft, diffused scent, an oil burner also adds the reassuringly cosy twinkle of a little flame as it burns, making it a lovely addition to a mantelpiece on winter evenings. It does need watching, though, as the combination of flame and hot oil is a little risky anywhere that it might be knocked over or reached by children or pets. You also need to take care not to let it burn dry.

 Naturally scented candles
A candle combines the cheerful flicker of a flame with the slow release of a fragrance and has the added benefit of looking beautiful when unlit, too. The choice out there is vast, with a range of candles available, from small votives to large glass jars. But again, these obviously need to be kept away from children when lit, so are best suited to rooms that don't get lots of through traffic.

Reed diffuser

Another way of releasing scent into a room without having to worry about candles or hot oil is to use a reed diffuser. This works by drawing up a scented solution from a glass jar via a bundle of thin reeds, which then releases a continuous stream of fragrance molecules into the air. To prevent any spillages, keep these on a high shelf or tucked away out of the reach of small hands and they will quietly and effectively perfume the air all day long.

 Fresh flowers

The original is always the best. So when you can, invest in the living, breathing version of your favourite floral scent, be it a vase of bluebells, an armful of roses or a branch of jasmine. The scent will be much subtler than an artificial replica, but it will be all the fresher and more delightful for it. Plus, if you pick flowers from your own garden, they will also bring something of the scent of the damp earth, fresh breeze or summer rain with them, which is something that really can't be bottled.

5 Fresh windowsill herbs in the kitchen

Mint, lemon balm, basil...if you love the zingy, uplifting scent of these common garden herbs, try growing containers of them in your kitchen or dining room so you can cut them fresh to make teas or flavour your cooking. I have a herb planter positioned near the door in my kitchen, as I like to gently brush my hand over the herbs on my way out in the morning to release the fresh, cheery scent.

6 Dried lavender

Brushing past a pot of fresh lavender is a wonderful way to get a delicate hit of that heady fragrance, but this is one flower that works almost as well in dried form. You can either buy a bag of dried lavender or make your own by hanging up a bunch of freshly cut stems indoors, somewhere warm, and letting them gently dry out. Once dried, lavender can be bagged up in little sachets and used to scent drawers and closets, or try tucking a small sachet of lavender in with your freshly laundered bed linen.

Linen spray

For freshly scented bedding, towels and throws, a naturally scented linen spray is a lovely way to bring your favourite scent into your living room or bedroom. Spritz onto textiles between washes to keep them fresh, or on laundry just before ironing. Soothing scents such as lavender can work wonderfully as a pillow mist before bed, too, if used sparingly.

> *"A freshly cooked loaf of bread or tray of cakes will create a cosy aroma, but if you lack the time or inclination to get baking, a vanilla candle or essential oil can have a similarly warming effect."*

Ready, steady, bake...

Who doesn't like the scent of freshly baked bread or cakes? Widely recommended by estate agents as a surefire way to make your home seem more appealing to potential buyers, the scent of home baking has something deeply reassuring and comforting about it. A freshly cooked loaf of bread or a tray of cakes will create a cosy aroma, but if you lack the time or inclination to get baking, a vanilla candle or essential oil can have a similarly warming effect.

Grow Your Own

While essential oils are a quick way to get a concentrated burst of fragrance at home, there are many scented plants that you can grow in your own garden, too, if you like the idea of a truly natural fragrance and have time to experiment. The following plants are all richly scented and some can even be grown in containers.

Garden plants

Mock orange (*Philadelphus*)

Jasmine (*Jasminum*)

Honeysuckle (*Lonicera*)

Roses (*Rosa*)

Eucalyptus (*Eucalyptus*)

Container plants

Lavender (*Lavandula*)

Rosemary (*Rosmarinus officinalis*)

Mint (*Mentha*)

Sweet peas (*Lathyrus odoratus*)

Hyacinth (*Hyacinthus*)

Right plant, right place

Repeat this mantra when choosing which flowers to grow in a bed or border. The key is to identify your soil type, note how much sun the area gets, then choose plants that will be happiest in those conditions. Ask at a local plant nursery for advice, or use an online tool such as the RHS Plant Finder. Alternatively, take a stroll around your neighbourhood and see which plants are growing well for your neighbours – chances are these will do well in your garden, too!

Cultivate containers

With container plants you can be a little more adventurous, as you can control the environment a bit more. So if you hanker after lavender but don't have the right soil conditions, plant up a large terracotta pot with a good potting mix and plenty of drainage. The flip side is that a container will need a little more love and attention than a border, as you have to be careful not to allow the soil to dry out or become too waterlogged.

6

Harness the Mood-Boosting Power of Flowers

There are few things that can lift my mood as quickly and effectively as a bunch of freshly picked garden flowers. From richly scented roses and delicate sweet peas to gently swaying stems of foxgloves and stately delphiniums, my home looks happier and my mood feels brighter when I take the time to fill a vase with flowers.

If you feel the same way, then there is a very good reason for that because these colourful little mood-enhancers have actually been scientifically proven to increase our happiness at home. According to one study at Rutgers University, New Jersey, published in *Evolutionary Psychology* journal, the presence of flowers has an immediate and long-term effect on emotional reactions, mood, social behaviours and even memory.

If you want to get a little of that flower power in your own home, here's how to harness some of that mood-boosting magic.

Petal Power:
How to Keep Your Flowers Alive for Longer

Part of the appeal of a bouquet of flowers is, for me, that the blooms have such a transient beauty. Watching a tightly closed flower bud unfurl into a deliciously scented rose over the course of a few short days, seeing it bloom into beauty and then gently fade, compels you to appreciate it fully during the few brief days that it is at its peak.

There are, however, a few ways to encourage your cut flowers to last that little bit longer indoors. I asked Stuart Fenwick, resident floral artist at bloomon, the flower delivery company, to share his top tips for keeping your flowers alive for as long as possible.

Don't hang about

Speed is the key when it comes to arranging cut flowers. You want to get them into a bucket of cool water as soon as possible, so when you get them home, immediately remove them from the packaging, cut the stems and plunge them into a bucket of cool water.

Cut stems at an angle

Cut 2.5cm (1in), at an angle, off your flower stems with a clean, sharp knife or pair of scissors; do this every time you change the water (see opposite), because the ends of the stems will quickly "seal up", preventing fresh water from being drawn up into the flower. Flowers or foliage with woody stems will need extra help to draw water up, so use a knife to slice the stem vertically up the centre, to maximize the surface area of the stem that has contact with the water.

Stay cool

Windowsills are common surfaces for displaying flowers but it is actually much better for your blooms to be kept out of direct sunlight and away from radiators or any other heat sources. That way, they will open at a slower rate and will last longer.

Add some bleach

A drop of bleach in the flower water will help to keep your flowers fresh by killing any bacteria. Change the water every three days and add a drop of bleach to prolong the life of your flowers. (Not too much, mind you – you want to kill the bacteria, not the flowers as well!)

Keep water levels low

It can be tempting to fill a vase to the brim with water, but this is actually detrimental to the life of your flowers, as it speeds up the rate at which the stems will start to deteriorate. Instead, just add a small amount of water to your vase. The only exception to this rule is if your bouquet contains woody stems (such as hedgerow berries); these need all the water they can get, so will appreciate a deep drink.

Strip excess leaves

Strip away any excess foliage from below the rim of the vase and make sure no leaves or foliage are submerged in the water, as this will lead to murky water and slimy flower stems.

Don't mix flowers with fruit

Flowers and fruit can look beautiful together, but actually they are not really the best of friends. Many fruits, including apples and pears, give off ethylene gas, which will make the flowers deteriorate, so keep your blooms well away from the fruit bowl if you want them to last longer indoors.

How to Arrange the Perfect Bouquet

Here are a few quick tips that will help you to create the perfect bouquet at home.

- Place your vase in front of you and use it to roughly measure each flower stem before you cut it.
- Strip away all the foliage that will sit below the neck of the vase (otherwise, this will quickly rot).
- Place your flowers in the vase one by one, at an angle, creating a tripod shape; turn your vase as you work so that you can view the bouquet from different angles.

- Vary the height of the flower stems to create movement and life (unless, of course, you are aiming for a tightly ordered arrangement of one type of flower displayed en masse).
- Place the tallest and sturdiest stems in the very centre of the vase to avoid the gap that can appear when less robust flower stems fall to the edges of the vase.

Blooming Lovely

Here's how to choose and arrange flowers to suit your interior style.

If your home is... contemporary

Stick to one colour

If your interior style is clean-lined and contemporary, stick to one colour of flower and go large with it to create a really striking display. Tall spikes of crimson red crocosmia would look wonderful in a simple glass vase, for example, as would a beautiful cluster of sky-blue delphiniums. The secret is to pick flowers with strong, clean lines and a saturated colour and give them the space to shine in their own right, without competition from other shapes and hues.

Choose structural foliage

It always pays to consider foliage if you want to create a sculptural display, so think about grasses and leaves as well as flower heads. Mix them in with flower stems or display them as sculptural forms in their own right. A bunch of eucalyptus stems always makes for a simple, elegant display and will give your room a beautifully fresh aroma, too.

> "If you want to make an impact, go large with your display and let it take centre stage."

Play with scale

A cluster of small flower arrangements can look whimsical and fun, but if you want to make an impact, go large with your display and let it take centre stage. An oversized vase filled with sculptural grasses, lush foliage and bold flower heads will shine in a minimal interior, and will usually be all the ornament you need to create impact in an entrance hallway or on a dining table.

Choose streamlined vases

Patterned vases or repurposed vessels, such as teacups, are perfect for a relaxed, country-style interior (see overleaf), but if you want to create a sleek display, steer clear of patterned or vintage-shaped vases and choose a large, streamlined vase instead, in either clear glass or a single block colour, for the greatest impact.

If your home is...country

Fill a ceramic jug
A glazed ceramic water jug in a bright, cheery colour is the perfect vessel for a country-style floral display. I have far too many of these in my own home, as I can't stop collecting them every time I see one for sale. Handmade ones are perfect, as they have that all-important "wobbly" appearance, and a hand-applied glaze or hand-painted finish also adds a dash of character.

Choose a mix of different-coloured wildflowers
Country-style is my personal favourite way of displaying flowers in my own home. I like to create a cheerful mix of different shapes, colours and sizes, drawing heavily on homegrown flowers or hedgerow finds, which tend to be more delicate and whimsical than hothouse flowers or shop-bought ones. A country-style flower display is the polar opposite of the neatly formal displays you tend to see in more traditional interiors, so use a variety of stem heights to create movement and life. Cottage-garden flowers such as foxgloves (*Digitalis*), lupins (*Lupinus*) and old-fashioned roses (*Rosa*) are the key to this look.

Celebrate hedgerow treasures
If you are able to forage locally without damaging wildlife habitats, there are treasures to be found in the hedgerow. I like to collect armfuls of frothy cow parsley (*Anthriscus sylvestris*) in the spring and branches of red and gold leaves and deep red berries in the autumn. Displaying local and seasonal finds such as these will help to anchor you to the landscape and stay in tune with the changing seasons.

Mix and match vases and containers
Country-style flower arranging is relaxed and free, so it lends itself beautifully to a mix-and-match approach to vases and containers. A cheery mix of teacups, cans and bottles filled with local flora and fauna will create a fun and happy display, so use whatever you have to hand and celebrate anything quirky, colourful or vintage in pattern and style.

> *"Use whatever you have to hand and celebrate anything quirky, colourful or vintage."*

If your home is...traditional

Fill a shallow bowl with roses

A cut-glass bowl filled with beautiful roses (*Rosa*) makes a chic, timeless floral display and is a quick way to enhance your interior. Perfect for placing on a formal hallway table alongside a cluster of shiny silver photo frames, or for adding a dash of understated glamour to a polished wood coffee table, this is a classic look that whispers elegance rather than shouts it.

Create large centrepiece displays

In a restful, neatly organized, traditional interior, small groups of containers can look messy and cluttered, so if you crave order and calm, create one large display rather than lots of little ones, and stick to a couple of types of flowers to prevent the display from having the "wild" look that is more at home in a country-style interior. Cream-coloured roses (*Rosa*), green and white hydrangea (*Hydrangea*) heads and straight-stemmed dahlias (*Dahlia*) are all classic flower choices for a restrained display.

Celebrate orchids

One flower that doesn't really need any clever arranging or further adornment is the orchid. These flowers ooze elegance and glamour and will add a layer of sophistication to any room they grace with their presence. Their sculptural form and glacial beauty are perfectly matched to a traditional interior. Try displaying a single orchid on a bedside table, or a cluster of three or five on a polished wood table as a show-stopping centrepiece.

> *"If you crave order and calm, try creating one large display rather than lots of little ones, and stick to a couple of types of flowers to prevent the display from having a 'wild' look."*

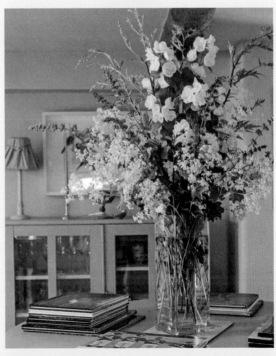

Six Vase Ideas That Won't Cost You a Penny

 Empty liquor bottles

I was on a flight with a friend recently when she ordered a gin and tonic. The miniature measure of gin arrived in the prettiest sky-blue bottle and as soon as it was empty I popped it in my hand luggage, because I knew it would make the cutest flower vase. And so it does. I use it in the winter to display the first of the tiny delicate snowdrops (*Galanthus*) and hellebores (*Helleborus*), and in the summer I fill it with delicate sweet peas (*Lathyrus odoratus*) or a couple of stems of lavender (*Lavandula*). Larger liquor bottles make excellent vases, too; gin, in particular, tends to come in wonderful green or blue glass bottles. Ask friends and family to save them for you or treat it as an excuse to throw a cocktail party and keep the empties.

Decorative tin cans

Some tins and cans are just too pretty to throw away, so make a point of saving any vintage-style containers or unusual food cans to reuse as flower vases. Old-fashioned olive oil cans or vintage mustard cans are unlikely but effective vases. Even humble tomato or baked bean cans can be requisitioned, too – just wash off the label if it isn't particularly appealing and give the metal beneath a coat of paint, or tie a length of pretty fabric or ribbon around it to liven it up.

Jam jars

Glass jars make ideal vases for small, country-style arrangements, and you can usually find one or two in every food cupboard. Give them a good scrub out when they are finished with, then fill them with a mix of pretty cottage-style flowers, cut short so the flower heads sit just above the rim. Twist some wire around the lip of the jar and curve it up and over to create a little handle, and you have created the perfect hanging vase for decorating an outdoor party.

Glass makeup bottles

Empty foundation bottles or glass perfume bottles make lovely little vases for mini bouquets. Perfume bottles, in particular, tend to be interesting shapes and beautiful colours, so a little cluster of them filled with a mix of small cottage-style flowers would make a lovely vintage-style display.

5 An ice bucket

If you need a large vase but don't have one to hand, an ice bucket can make an excellent stand-in. They usually have straight sides or flare out slightly at the top, so are ideal for holding a large bunch of tall flowers and creating a dramatic centrepiece.

6 Teacups

Delicate vintage teacups are perfect for displaying old-fashioned blowsy roses; a cluster of mismatched floral-patterned teacups filled with large scented roses would make a whimsical display for a summer tea party. You will need to cut the stems very short for this and you may also need to fix them in place with a grid of tape (see below for details), but they will lend a pretty elegance to your table.

TOP TIP

If you have a wide-necked vase or bowl and you're struggling to keep your flower arrangement looking neat, here's a secret florists' tip to keep your blooms in place. Using a roll of slim masking tape, make a grid across the top of the container by laying strips of tape horizontally and then vertically from one side of the rim to the other. This way you will create a neat grid of little squares that you can use as a framework to hold your flowers. Start to build your display by posting individual stems into the gaps between the tape to structure the whole display by keeping each bloom firmly but gently in place.

How to Grow Your Own

If you want to have a cheap and local supply of flowers all year round, why not grow a few of your own? You don't need a huge garden for this; in fact, you don't even need a garden, because many flowers can be grown in patio containers or balcony plant pots.

I asked Professor Alistair Griffiths, Director of Science & Collections at the Royal Horticultural Society (RHS), which plants he would suggest as the easiest to grow for total beginners and he recommended a simple mix of four different bulbs (see below). The fact that they are perennial bulbs means they will come up year after year in a container, so once you have planted them you can just let them get on with it.

Perennial bulbs for a year-round flower supply

Spring: daffodils (*Narcissus*)
There are few sights more cheering than the first daffodils of spring, heralding the return of warmer days.

Summer: purple alliums (*Allium*)
These large purple flowers make a really striking display in a summer garden and are wonderful as a cut flower to take indoors, too.

Autumn: crocuses (*Crocus*)
For a mood-boosting splash of colour just as the rest of the garden is fading, plant a cluster of autumn-flowering crocus bulbs during the summer months.

Winter: snowdrops (*Galanthus*)
Planting just a few snowdrop bulbs in late spring will reward you with little points of brilliant white light the following winter.

Shine a Light on Wellbeing

There is one very unlikely room in my home that I have ended up using almost more than any other. The reason for this has everything to do with the subject of this chapter. The room in question is a tiny little guest room at the back of the house, but from midday onward on a sunny day it is bathed in the warmest golden sunshine. When the doors are open, the birds are singing and the trees are gently swaying outside, it is a glorious, peaceful, sun-drenched space. It is my favourite place to be. This chapter should provide some inspiration on the best ways to bring the sunshine indoors.

Can Natural Light Make Us Happier and Healthier?

The mood-boosting qualities of this little room made me wonder if the amount of natural daylight we get in our homes has a direct correlation to our mood, happiness and general wellbeing. I decided to see if I could uncover any proven links between daylight levels at home and health and happiness levels. To help me do so, I spoke to Dr Phyllis Zee, director of Sleep Medicine at Northwestern Medicine in Chicago, Illinois, who has undertaken research into this very topic in collaboration with the University of Illinois.

Dr Zee found that office workers with more light exposure in the workplace had longer sleep duration, better sleep quality, more physical activity and a better quality of life compared to office workers with less light exposure in the workplace. So do these findings carry over into our homes? "We studied the office environment because we spend so much of the daytime indoors at work," Dr Zee explained to me, "but yes, the same theory applies to homes." So why exactly does daylight have such a big impact on our health? "Light is the most important time giver for internal timing," says Dr Zee, "and thus can positively or negatively affect health – depending on the time of exposure."

Good day sunshine!

According to Dr Zee's research, timing is everything when it comes to light levels in the home, and morning light can have a huge impact on our health and happiness. "Morning light has been shown to be particularly important for mood, sleep and weight regulation," she says. "If possible, you should try to sit or work next to a window in the morning," advises Dr Zee, "and have breakfast near a window."

If this really isn't possible, the next best alternative is to "install artificial lighting (white broad-spectrum) that is bright in areas that are most frequented". Light should be about 1000 lux, according to Dr Zee, and you can measure this with a light meter, or even with some smartphones.

Wind down naturally

"While light exposure in the morning and during the day is beneficial," says Dr Zee, "exposure during the evening is actually detrimental to sleep, and perhaps metabolism." To help your body to wind down naturally and prepare for sleep, Dr Zee suggests you start to dim your lights at home from about 8pm (on light summer evenings, start to draw the curtains). "This is the time that for most people, their own melatonin, produced by the pineal gland, begins to rise, to help signal darkness to the body," she explains. "Bright light exposure late in the evening will block secretion of this natural hormone of darkness."

(To find out more about how to create the perfect environment for sleep, take a look at pages 48–61.)

"Timing is everything when it comes to light levels in the home, and morning light can have a huge impact on our health and happiness."

Let There Be Light:

Nine Ways to Flood Your Home with Mood-boosting Sunlight

Most people feel better with the warmth of the sun on their face, so here's how to maximize the amount of natural daylight in your home.

Reflect light with mirrors

Mirrors can work magic in a dark interior, so hang them liberally on your walls and watch your daylight double. Place them opposite a sunny window to reflect light, or on a wall directly underneath a skylight to magnify the effect. Mirrors also work particularly well in a dark, narrow hallway and it can pay to choose the largest one you can afford for this typically dark and sunless space. If your budget is tight, you could have a piece of mirror cut to size by a glass specialist. This will often work out to be more cost-effective than buying a regular mirror, if you need to cover a large area, and you can usually choose from a range of finishes, from crystal clear to delicately "foxed" (which is the name for that beautifully marbled finish you see on antique mirrors). You can also help to scatter sunlight by choosing a faceted mirror, or add an unexpected twist with a wall of reflective mirrored tiles in a kitchen or bathroom.

> *"Mirrors can work magic in a dark interior, so hang them liberally on your walls and watch your daylight double."*

② Choose a front door with a glass panel

A heavy front door will, obviously, block all light from entering your home, but replacing it with a glass-panelled door can transform a dark hallway and draw extra daylight into a gloomy interior. If you are worried about privacy, choose frosted or etched glass for the panels and pull a curtain across at night-time. Stained-glass panels are a beautiful option for a front door, as they have the power to transform daylight as it travels through from outside to inside. I saw a beautiful stained-glass panel designed in a sunburst pattern in a house I visited several years ago. As light filtered through the yellow and orange glass panels from outside, it was transformed into beams of rich golden sunlight that flooded the narrow hallway beyond.

③ Clear cluttered windowsills

Sweep clutter off your windowsills and scrub them clean to allow as much light to flood inside as possible. It may sound like a small change, but you would be surprised how much a windowsill display of photo frames, vases or ornaments can eat into the window space and reduce the amount of light filtering through.

So place your ornaments elsewhere and polish the windowsills to a shine to ensure maximum light reflection. Another obvious but easy fix for increasing sunlight in an interior is to ensure your windows are sparklingly clean. Give them a regular scrub to counteract the build-up of dirt and grime and the quality of light should improve.

4 Replace solid interior doors with glass-panelled ones

An open-plan layout is the obvious way to maximize natural daylight indoors, but if that is not an option, there are several ways to achieve the same effect without getting demolition-happy. Swapping solid interior doors for glass ones is an easy way to allow light to filter through from one room to the next while still providing a clear division. Internal windows are another option and are worth asking your architect or builder to consider if you are about to start any renovation work. The aim of these is to connect both sides of the house and allow light to make its way from one side to the other. This is rare in most homes because internal walls, doors or hallways usually block the centre of the space. But if you can connect rooms – either front to back or side to side – with glass doors or windows, it will allow sunshine to travel from one to the other as the sun moves overhead throughout the day, allowing the darker room to "borrow" daylight from the sunnier one in the morning, and vice versa in the evening.

5 Try a light tunnel or solar tube

To increase luminosity in a dark room with little or no natural light, a solar tube or light tunnel can be a very effective option and an alternative to installing artificial light. Ideal for a basement, hallway or internal room with no outward-facing windows, they can funnel light down from outside and flood a dark room with daylight. Again, these are probably only an option to consider if you are about to start renovation work, but they really can transform a windowless space, so ask your architect or builder about the possibility of adding one.

6 Open up the stairs

Top floors will be brighter than lower floors in many houses, so think about how you can pull some of this natural light down via your staircase. Choosing open-riser stairs will allow slivers of light to make their way down from upper floors. Alternatively, painting your stair treads in a light-toned paint is another way to help bounce light down each step to lower floors. Mirrors, again, are useful here, and a mirrored staircase wall will work wonders in reflecting light from upper floors and directing it down into the rest of the house. If you are about to undertake a redesign, adding a light well to a staircase can be a very effective way of brightening up a gloomy stairwell and shining light down into lower floors, so ask your architect or builder if this could be an option.

7 Hang curtains so they pull right away from the window when open

A secret interior designers' tip when hanging drapes is to choose a curtain pole that extends out beyond the window frame, so when you draw the curtains back you pull them clear of the window and they rest against the wall instead. This allows you to keep the entire width of the window clear and will ensure maximum daylight gets in. The same goes for blinds – choose ones that pull up and away from the window, rather than allowing them to sit low within the window frame and blocking light from entering.

8 Choose reflective materials

As well as mirrors, many other materials have light-reflecting qualities, so consider bringing some of these into your room scheme to help scatter more light around. This doesn't have to mean lots of hard-edged materials like glass and metal, though; gloss paint finishes, metallic frames, highly polished wood surfaces and light-coloured flooring will all help to maximize every scrap of daylight that makes its way into the room. Dark colours and matt textures will have the opposite effect, so save those for spaces where you want to engender a feeling of dark, cocooning cosiness.

9 Look to the sky

If you are overshadowed by other buildings or if your windows are not quite pulling in the amount of light you would like, a roof light could be your new best friend. Rather than relying on a few hours of sunlight each day, an overhead roof light will offer more hours of consistent daylight than regular windows can provide. By pulling light directly down from above, the light quality is often much better than that supplied by a vertical window, too. They are also great options for a side-return extension, a single-storey building or a loft conversion.

Liven It Up:
Three Ways to Brighten a Gloomy View

Sometimes, however, with the best will in the world, it is not possible to throw your windows open, or even have them uncovered for large parts of the day. Unappealing views or privacy concerns in urban areas can mean that you need to keep your windows screened all day long. If that is the case in your home, don't worry, just pick one of the following window treatments to protect your privacy while still allowing the daylight in.

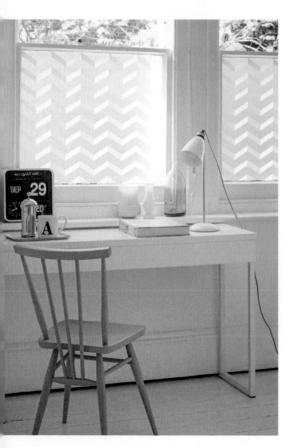

1 Clever window film

Window film is a great, low-cost choice for screening a window while still letting natural light through. There are lots of fun options available, from bespoke designs to patterns you can order by the metre or yard, and they are a good way to add personality to a room. When I redecorated my bathroom I wanted to replace the roller blinds, which were cutting into the window space, so I installed a window film with a subtle metallic finish instead. The film has tiny silver particles embedded in it which lend a dazzling luminosity to the light as it filters through. I chose a design flecked with tiny cutout stars, which allow small slivers of light to glint through and scatter pinpoints of sunshine around the room in the morning. For such a little amount of money, this window treatment has absolutely transformed the small space, so it's a great option if you are short of time or funds. It's also an ideal solution for a rented home, as it's easy to install and remove.

Smart shutters

2 Shutters with adjustable louvres are useful if you want to control the light or privacy levels in a room through the day, because they can be opened or closed as required and angled to let the light in while still providing privacy from outside. They also look effortlessly smart and you can choose from a range of colours and finishes, including natural wood, classic white, bright primaries and soft pastels. Choose light colours for maximum reflective powers, and a glossy finish for extra luminosity.

Sheer fabric

3 If you prefer the flutter of a curtain at your window, a sheer light-coloured linen is a good option for screening a window without completely blocking the light. A lightweight, open-weave fabric will draw a soft veil over an unattractive view or screen your interior from people walking past while allowing a diffused light to filter through. A soft fabric will also flutter very pleasingly in the breeze if the window is open, so it is a good way to bring life and movement to a gloomy space.

"A soft fabric will flutter very pleasingly in the breeze if the window is open."

Follow the Sun:

How to Design Your Rooms Around the Direction of Sunlight

Often we accept our floor plans and room layouts as fixed entities when we move into a new home, without stopping to think if they are the best solutions for us. But with this new knowledge about the power of sunlight, it could be time to overhaul your floor plan and shake up your room layouts.

Consider for a moment the way the sun travels, rising in the east and setting in the west. In terms of your home, that means an east-facing room will get the sunlight first thing in the morning, while a west-facing room will remain in shade, and vice versa in the evening. So far, so logical. But do you use the rooms in a way that makes the most of this or are you fighting against it without realizing?

> *"An east-facing room will get the sunlight first thing in the morning, while a west-facing room will remain in shade, and vice versa in the evening."*

For example, in an ideal world you would start your day in an east-facing room, to make the most of the morning sunlight, and then move to a west-facing room later in the day, to bask in the mellow, late-afternoon sunshine. While it might not be possible to drastically alter the layout of your home, take a look at your floor plans and consider if there are any small tweaks you could make to enable you to follow the sun around your home. Is it possible to eat breakfast in an east-facing room, for example? Could you move your evening sitting room to a west-facing space?

North, east, south or west...which is best?

Here's how to chase the sun.

In the Northern hemisphere, North-facing rooms tend to get a cooler, blue-toned natural light, so try to allocate them for areas that get the least use, such as utility rooms, bathrooms or storage spaces. (This applies to south-facing rooms in the Southern hemisphere.)

East-facing rooms tend to have "warmer" light in the mornings and "colder" light in the evenings, so are ideal for breakfast rooms or bedrooms, if you like to wake up with the sun.

South-facing rooms (in the Northern hemisphere) usually get the highest levels of warm natural light, so it makes sense to use them for living spaces and family rooms to really make the most of them.

West-facing rooms tend to feel colder in the mornings and warmer in the evenings as the sun travels, so these are perfect for evening living spaces.

8

How to Create a Cosy Retreat

One of the cosiest memories I can recall is of curling up in front of a large open fire, watching the flames dance and flicker, feeling the warmth on my face and listening to the soft rise and fall of family chatter all around. This feeling of cosiness and contentment had as much to do with being surrounded by the security and comfort of family as it did with the crackle of the logs in the grate, the warmth of the flames and the softness of the rug beneath me.

So it is that in my view a "cosy" room has to have three essential elements: warmth, texture and security. Security, for me, is the feeling of being safe and surrounded by close friends and family, while warmth and texture can be anything from cosy lighting and soft materials to the snug cocoon of a cosy reading nook. In this chapter I have looked at ways of increasing the cosy factor at home and creating a space that nourishes and nurtures.

Staying In Is the New Going Out:

Five Quick Ways to Create a Cosy Home on a Budget

Create a sense of ease and relaxation at home with these simple updates to warm up your interior and bring in tactile layers.

> *"Use a variety of different tactile elements that will pull together to create a soft, enveloping space in which to hibernate as the nights draw in."*

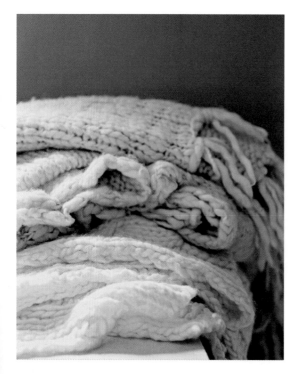

1 Choose natural textures

The secret to a cosy room scheme is to use a variety of different tactile elements that will pull together to create a soft, enveloping space in which to hibernate as the nights draw in. Steer clear of anything hard-edged or cold, such as metal, glass or concrete, and choose soft, natural materials instead, to create a room scheme that invites you to settle in and relax. Everything that you use on a daily basis should be made of simple but good-quality materials, so when you are choosing a new throw, cushion or even a mug, think about how the material feels as well as how it looks. Polished wood, hand-glazed pottery, crisp cottons and soft linens are all worth investing in, and any materials that you have frequent contact with, such as door handles or light pulls, for example, should be considered carefully, too.

2 Layer up

The key to staying warm on a chilly day is to dress yourself in several thin layers, so think of your home in the same way – and layer, layer, layer. In your living room, drape a soft throw over the arm of your sofa so you can easily reach for it if the temperature drops, and pile up a couple of large, soft cushions to snuggle into. Add in a thick pair of woollen socks and a mug of something warm and you are approaching perfection. In your bedroom, try layering crisp linen sheets with a plump cotton or velvet blanket, or keep a soft wool throw folded over the foot of the bed for extra warmth.

3 Create pools of light

A bright, overhead strip light or LED spotlights will create clear, functional light for cooking or working under at home, but when you want to switch to cosy mode, you should choose warm-toned yellow light and build up soft layers of it. The aim is to create a welcoming wash of light, so bring in a couple of table lamps and floor lamps to build up a patchwork of warm light. Choose warm-toned lightbulbs or select lampshades with a rich gold or yellow interior to create a cocooning circle of golden light (see also page 26).

4 String it out

Strings of twinkling lights can create a warming effect if you choose ones with yellow-toned bulbs, rather than brilliant-white bulbs. Pile them up in a large glass jar to create a diffused glow or weave them around an unlit fireplace to give the illusion of warmth. You can also twist ropes of small lights along the top of a cupboard or shelf and they will scatter tiny points of warm light around the room.

5 Treat your toes

If you have hardwood, tile or laminate flooring, you will need to warm it up quickly when the temperature drops, so a thick-pile rug is your best friend here. Choose the softest ones you can find and place them anywhere your bare feet might hit the chilly ground, such as beside the bed or sofa. The secret to choosing the best rug is always to buy the largest one you can afford; a common mistake is to opt for a little square of a rug and place it directly in front of a chair. If a large rug is out of your budget (and they can be pricey), then build up a patchwork of smaller, cheaper rugs to create the effect of one large one. Run this right underneath the sofa or bed and it will have the effect of "anchoring" the furniture and making the room look larger, as well as dramatically upping the cosy factor.

Ten Lessons to Learn from the Danes

The Danes are widely held up as the happiest nation in the world, and much has been made of their concept of "hygge" – the word for creating an atmosphere that is cosy and snug. It is interesting to consider, however, that the concept of hygge came out of a country that is also renowned for its love of minimalism and of clean, pared-back, monochrome interiors. So how do the two knit together, and does this hold the key to cosiness? I asked Danish design journalist Kasper Iversen to shed some light on it.

The secret to hygge

"It can seem as if there's a conflict between hygge and Scandi minimalism, as on the surface many elements seem completely opposite," agrees Kasper. "Hygge is about cosiness, whereas minimalism is about clearing out everything that's not absolutely essential." But he believes there is a common thread between the two and it is *this* that holds the key to the Danish way of life.

"Both hygge and minimalism embody a desire to keep things simple and uncomplicated," he says. "Minimalism is about not having more than you need, and hygge is about enjoying life through simple pleasures." So if you keep simplicity in mind when creating your home, you are on the way to discovering what makes Danes so happy. "Don't make it complicated," Kasper says, "don't make it stressful. That's the secret to the Danish way of life and the secret to hygge."

Here are Kasper's top tips for creating a simple "hygge" atmosphere at home.

Choose natural textiles

Textiles should be natural, hard-wearing and unpretentious in order to create a sense of hygge at home. "The key thing to ask yourself is 'will it be ruined by a spilled drink?'" says Kasper. If you are worried about expensive fabrics being ruined, then you won't be able to truly relax, so choose washable cotton and linen slipcovers for sofas and armchairs, and steer clear of delicate silks and expensive velvets, as "these are really not hygge".

2 Cook simple meals

"Formal dining can never be hygge," says Kasper. The aim is to create a relaxed, cosy atmosphere, so the last thing you want to worry about is cooking a complicated or pretentious dinner that makes you anxious. Make something simple that you have cooked many times before and focus on spending time with your guests, rather than fussing over a hot stove in the kitchen.

3 Create cosy lighting

"You don't want your lighting to be too bright," says Kasper. So to create a welcoming and enveloping feel at home, layer up warm, yellow-toned light sources, such as table or floor lamps, and avoid bright overhead lights. Oh, and of course, bring in candlelight for ultimate hygge.

4 Light a candle

Does the amount of hygge correlate to the number of candles you light? I put the question to Kasper, who advised moderation. "By all means, light one or two candles to create atmosphere, but don't go out and buy 30 candles because you think that is what's expected," he says. "Just use what you have to hand and what you think is cosy."

5 Bake it to make it

"Hygge is a feeling," says Kasper, so you need to consider all the senses when creating a cosy atmosphere, and scent is an important one. "Hygge is like a home-baked cake," he says – a warm, comforting scent that typifies a lazy afternoon spent indoors. So if you want to get that cosy, nostalgic feeling for yourself, ramp up the cosy scents with a fresh loaf of bread or a vanilla cake.

"You need to consider all the senses when creating a cosy atmosphere."

6 Take your time

You can't hurry hygge. "It's all about being relaxed," says Kasper, "so you can't hygge if you're feeling stressed or in a rush." Don't put too much pressure on yourself by trying to entertain too many people, or by organizing anything too elaborate. Keep things simple and uncomplicated and allow yourself plenty of time to ease into a relaxed and mellow mindset.

7 Buy one good cake

"If you've invited friends over for coffee, there's no need to worry about buying lots of different treats for your guests," says Kasper. "Just buy one type of pastry that you really love and serve that – keep it simple and easy."

8 Put down roots

"Wood is very hygge," says Kasper. It's a natural material, so it's much softer than hard-edged surfaces, such as glass or concrete, and will help to create a relaxed, hygge atmosphere at home. "It's a down-to-earth material," says Kasper, so bring in a wooden table, wooden dining chairs or even wooden accessories, such as candlesticks or bowls, to create a warm and welcoming home environment.

9 Focus on friendship

Spending time with people you like and feel comfortable with is at the heart of hygge. "Hygge is something you can only do with people you feel relaxed around," agrees Kasper. So an evening spent with close friends or family is perfect. Inviting someone over with the express purpose of impressing them is the polar opposite of hygge, as is spending time with someone that you feel anxious around, so focus on your close friends and family and those that you can totally relax with.

10 Embrace imperfection

"Trying too hard to make something 'perfect' is stressful and not relaxing, so it goes against the concept of hygge," Kasper says. Don't try to create what you think others consider perfect; keep things simple instead and give yourself permission to fashion an environment that you like and that makes you feel happy. "The 'perfect' home is the one where you feel comfortable," says Kasper. So whether you are having a simple meal around your kitchen table or a cup of coffee and a catch-up with a friend, don't fuss about producing the perfect event. If your dinner plates are mismatched or the meal doesn't turn out quite as you planned, it doesn't matter, so embrace the imperfections.

The Joy of Candles, Real Fires and Wood-burners:

How to Fill Your Home with Warmth

A roaring fire on a dark winter's evening will hold a magnetic draw for everyone in a room, and once you get a cheerful blaze going you'll find that competition is fierce for the closest seat to the hearth. Even a rug in front of the fireplace can be considered prime position for stretching out before the flames and daydreaming. It is the ultimate in cosiness, listening to the comforting crackle and whisper of the log fire.

Whether you are lucky enough to have an open fire in your home or not, there are several ways to bring the flickering warmth and caveman-cosiness of fire into your living space. Here's how.

Focus on the fire

There is something beautifully mesmerizing about the dancing flames and happy crackle of a log fire, and if you are lucky enough to have an open fire or wood-burning stove in your living space, you absolutely need to give it the attention it deserves. Get it cleaned out and in top working condition and start thinking of it as the centrepiece of your room. Often the TV gets all the consideration in a living room and becomes the focal point for the arrangement of furniture. However, to design the cosiest room possible, forget about the TV for a moment. Think instead of the fireplace as the centre of attention, to which you want to direct your gaze in the evening, and ensure the flames can be seen (and the warmth felt) from every seating position in the room. Make sure the fire is easy to light, which means keeping the hearth freshly swept, the fire ready-laid and a stack of firewood close by, so as soon as there is the slightest chill in the air you can simply put a match to it and get a blaze going in no time.

"There is something beautifully mesmerizing about the dancing flames and happy crackle of a log fire."

Fill a fireplace

If you have a decorative fireplace, rather than a working one, you can still create the effect of a cheerful log fire by filling the fireplace with a cluster of church candles to mimic the dancing warmth of a real fire. Alternatively, fill an empty fireplace with a stack of freshly chopped logs and weave a string of lights in between, to create a twinkling focal point and bring a little of the warmth and fragrance of firewood into your living space.

Branch out

Firelight can bring warmth and life to other rooms in your home, too, so consider bringing the cheerful glow of a candle into your kitchen, dining room or bathroom. A simple candlestick on a kitchen table will add atmosphere and cosy warmth to mealtimes, while a couple of candles in glass jars in a bathroom

will engender a cocooning spa-like feel at bath times. If you are worried about the risk of fire, create a safety candle by placing a small votive candle in a glass jar filled with sand or even water (it will float on top), and the candle will extinguish itself when it has burned down; but never, ever leave a candle burning when there is no one in the room.

How to Create a Reading Nook

Give me a good book and a comfy chair and I am very happy. My idea of cosy perfection is a dedicated reading nook, piled up with deep, comfy cushions and surrounded by stacks of books. If you would like to squeeze a dedicated reading space into your home, here are four ways to create your own library nook.

1 **Take over a corner**
Is there a quiet corner in your home that you can requisition as a reading spot? The key is to choose somewhere peaceful and, ideally, away from the main living room. It doesn't have to be a large space; the best reading nooks are snug and cosy, so as long as there is enough space to tuck in a chair and a lamp, then it will work. Potentially overlooked corners to consider are hallway landings, guest bedrooms or dining rooms, so get your creative thinking hat on and look at your home with fresh eyes to locate the perfect "nook".

2 **Transform a cupboard**
This might sound a little unusual, but a cupboard can actually make an ideal reading nook. If you are able to clear out a hallway, bedroom or playroom cupboard, you then just need to take down any internal shelves and remove the door and you have an instant cocoon-like den. Pile up plenty of comfy floor cushions, install some good, welcoming lighting and you have created the perfect reading nook for children. Or, if you have a little more time and budget and want to create a grown-up reading nook, ask a carpenter to build a raised seating bench into the cupboard space and line it with plump cushions to create a cosy retreat where you can hide away from the hustle and bustle of daily life.

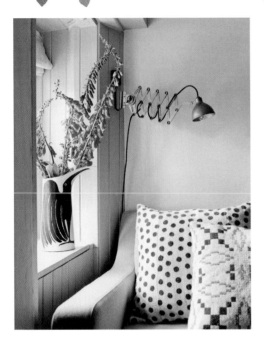

③ Light it right

To create the perfect cosy corner you will want to avoid really bright overhead lighting, but you do need good enough light to read by and avoid eyestrain. A wall-mounted reading lamp is perfect for a cupboard nook and a floor lamp will do the trick in a cosy corner. For a children's reading nook, try stringing ropes of lights across the ceiling of the space to create a magical, den-like atmosphere, in addition to a dedicated reading light.

> *"My idea of cosy perfection is a dedicated reading nook, piled up with deep, comfy cushions and surrounded by stacks of books."*

④ Be inspired by Harry Potter

The awkward triangle of cupboard space under the stairs is often used for little more than coat or shoe storage (or housing the occasional child wizard), but it can actually be the perfect space for a reading nook. Removing the stud wall, if there is one, and slotting in a low bench or chair, a reading lamp and heaps of soft cushions can turn the space from an underutilized dust trap into a magical reading spot. Use the tallest end of the space to install your seating and the tricky, narrow end of the wedge to tuck in a few bookshelves – that way, you will make the most of every scrap of floor space and create a fun hideaway for children and adults alike.

9

Wish Happiness for Others

A few years ago, an engineer called Chade-Meng Tan started to research ways to increase levels of happiness and emotional intelligence at work. The programme he developed, Search Inside Yourself, was initially just for his colleagues, but it is now a globally recognized programme. It has a very simple secret to happiness at its heart. The key to improving your own sense of wellbeing, says Tan, is to practice compassion. In other words, if you wish other people to be happy, you will become happier too.

The Secret Is Out

In many ways it seems counterintuitive to look for happiness for yourself by wishing it for others, but the more I thought about it, the more it made sense. There is a certain selfless pleasure to be found in acts of generosity, and taking the focus outside of yourself, to consider others instead, is bound to have a trickle-down effect on your own levels of joy or contentment. So, by wishing others to be happy and acting on the impulse to be generous with your time and love, you can, in return, bask in the reflected glow of their happiness.

An independent scientific study led by Soyoung Q. Park at the Department of Economics at the University of Zurich seems to back this up, too. In an experiment to test the link between generosity and happiness, two groups of volunteers were given a sum of money – half were told to spend it on a treat for themselves and half were told to spend it on a treat for someone else. Those that spent the money on others were discovered to have higher levels of happiness as a result.

> *"Taking the focus outside of yourself, to consider others instead, is bound to have a trickle-down effect on your own levels of joy or contentment."*

Mood Boosters

Generosity doesn't just have to involve money, though. Sometimes, small acts of kindness and thoughtfulness are just as, if not more, effective as going out and buying a gift for someone. Here are eight ways to consider the happiness of others and share a little love.

1 **Cook someone their favourite meal**
Taking the time to prepare and cook someone their favourite meal will earn you heaps of brownie points while spreading a little happiness – I know I am always ridiculously grateful if someone offers to cook for me. So if you have culinary skills, share them widely and freely.

"There is a certain selfless pleasure to be found in acts of generosity."

2 **Send thank-you letters**
Handwritten thank-you letters are a joy to receive, so take the time to write them to friends and family after every birthday or Christmas. Treat yourself to some beautiful notepaper or some pretty cards and make sure you send them promptly after someone sends you a gift or does something nice for you. In particular, encourage children to remember to send thank-you notes to older relatives.

3 Invite someone for the holidays if you know they don't have family nearby

If you hear that a work friend or neighbour will be spending the holidays or a weekend alone, invite them over to share a meal with you and involve them in your own family's celebrations. If they don't have their own family nearby, they might be delighted to be invited to join in with your festivities. If you feel shy about inviting them, don't be; they can easily say a polite no if they would rather be alone, but even just offering is an act of kindness in itself.

4 Do someone else's chores for them

If you notice that someone is having a really bad week, sprinkle a little happiness by doing a couple of their chores for them. I know that if someone offered to do the vacuuming and cleaning for me one week, I would be over the moon, so I can vouch for the effectiveness of this one.

5 Sort through your clothes and give everything you no longer wear to charity

If you have clothes, shoes or bags gathering dust in the back of your wardrobe, have a good clear-out and take everything that you no longer wear to your local charity shop or thrift store (see page 40). Enabling someone else to benefit from something you no longer need is easy, and will give you a little glow of satisfaction.

6 Bake a cake for someone

If you make an excellent lemon drizzle cake and you know it's your flatmate's favourite, don't wait until their birthday to make them one – surprise them with it on an ordinary weekday or whenever you think they might need a little boost.

"Make the effort to say out loud every time you notice something good about someone."

7 Compliment someone

Taking the time to notice your flatmate's new haircut is a tiny thing for you to remember to do, but it could give them a big confidence boost, so make the effort to say out loud every time you notice something good about someone. Make it a habit to vocalize positive or generous thoughts and you will spread a warm glow of happiness and confidence wherever you go.

8 Spend time with older relatives

If you have older relatives who live alone, invite them over for dinner, ask them about themselves and listen to their stories. In the hustle and bustle of everyday life it can be easy to overlook spending time with aunts, uncles or grandparents, but they are the closest link you have to your own history, so take the time to treat them with kindness and respect and you will gain as much, if not more, from the interaction.

Everybody Needs Good Neighbours

Where better to start in your quest to wish happiness for others than in your own community? I am lucky enough to live in a wonderful village where the concept of being a good neighbour is highly prized. The street I live on is particularly tightknit and my lovely neighbours generously sprinkle small kindnesses around. They keep an eye on the house for me when I am out at work, put my garbage bins out for collection when I forget and are always there for a chat if I need them to be. If you want to create a similar street spirit, treat your neighbours as you would your own family and, I promise, you will get as much, if not more, happiness back as you put in. Here are eight ways to be a good neighbour.

Offer to cut next-door's lawn

If you live in a terrace or row of houses with adjoining lawns, offer to mow next-door's grass when you cut your own. If they aren't keen on doing this job themselves, they may well be delighted, and they might even return the favour for you one day. But do check first – keen gardeners might not take kindly to this.

Welcome new neighbours to the street

Moving home can be a stressful experience and it often falls to the new neighbours to introduce themselves to the existing residents of the street, which can be a bit nerve-wracking. Make it easier for any new neighbours by popping a welcome card through the door when they arrive and by making the effort to say hello to them first.

Start a book exchange library

There is an unused telephone box in my village that has been converted into a neighbourhood lending library. It runs on an honesty system, whereby anyone can take a book for free and replace it with a book they no longer want or need. I absolutely love it and it is a very simple thing to set up. If there isn't an obvious communal area in your street for this, try a small weatherproof book box in your front garden, or turn an American-style mailbox into a mini lending library.

"Where better to start in your quest to wish happiness for others than in your own community?"

Support local events

If your local school, church or choir holds a summer fair or puts on a Christmas play, make the effort to go along and support it. A lot of time and effort can go into local events and if only a handful of people turn up, it can be a little dispiriting for all those who volunteer their time to make these events happen. Turning up and joining in is a simple act of kindness that is also a great way to meet your neighbours and show your support. Who knows, you might discover a surprising aptitude for choral singing along the way.

Make a handmade card

When I was a child my sisters and I always used to make handmade birthday cards for our elderly next-door neighbour. One year we ran out of time, so we sent her a regular shop-bought card instead. When we saw her next she thanked us for the card but declared that she preferred the wobbly, glue-and-glitter-covered handmade ones we had sent her in previous years and she produced a box filled with every card we had ever made her, which she had carefully kept. So after that, we reverted to making her a birthday card every year. If you have an elderly neighbour who would appreciate a handmade card, take the time to make one, or help your children to make one.

Offer to look after your neighbour's home/pets/plants while they are away

If your neighbours are planning a summer break, offer to keep an eye on their home for them while they are away to help put their minds at rest. Whether that involves collecting the mail, watering their prize tomato plants or feeding their goldfish, it's a small gesture of the type that can really help community life to blossom. Plus, your grateful neighbours might well offer to help you in exchange the next time you go away.

Share skills

Do you have a secret skill? Perhaps you are a guerrilla knitter, or maybe you are a champion banjo player? If so, don't keep it to yourself, but offer your skills to anyone in your street who you think might be keen to learn. This doesn't mean you have to put a sign up in the window, or take your banjo from door to door to spread the word. But if someone expresses an interest in a hobby of yours, offering to teach them or sharing some of your time or materials to get them started is a very kind thing to do.

Post Christmas cards (or cookies) by hand

I always try to pop a Christmas card through the door of my closest neighbours each year – it is a fun way to keep in touch and I love to receive cards back, too. I also like to bake, so I make a batch of festive gingerbread biscuits and, around a week or so before the holidays, I deliver them along the street. It is a nice way to chat to neighbours who, perhaps, I haven't seen for a while, and the biscuits usually seem to be well received (or my neighbours are too polite to say otherwise). It is a simple thing to do and it makes me feel happy and festive to think that I am handing out a little bit of Christmas cheer along with the gingerbread.

It Takes Two

Relationships are essential for our happiness at home, and taking the time to cultivate strong relationships with your family, your partner or your flatmates is crucial when you are all sharing a living space. A major ongoing research project undertaken by the Harvard Study of Adult Development has followed hundreds of men for nearly 80 years (they started the study in 1938) and found that close relationships, more than money or fame, are what keep people happy throughout their lives. They found that close ties to others help to delay mental and physical decline, and are better predictors of long and happy lives than social class, IQ or even genes. Here's how to build up your relationships at home.

Design your living room for conversation

It is too easy to design your living area around the TV, and many of us fall into the trap of doing this. But if you think instead about designing your living room for conversation, you will be much more likely to use the space for chatting and relaxing, rather than just watching TV as a default behaviour. All it might take is a simple design tweak, such as angling two sofas to look at each other, rather than having them both facing the TV, or making sure that each family member has their own dedicated space in a living room, so they will feel comfortable and want to spend time there instead of disappearing to their own room every evening.

> *"Close relationships, more than money or fame, are what keep people happy throughout their lives."*

Share meals at the dinner table

Sitting at the table to eat dinner together is a good way to make sure that you take time to talk properly at least once a day. So if your kitchen table tends to be a magnet for clutter and you find yourself grabbing meals on the go or in front of the TV, make a point of keeping the table clear so you can sit down properly to eat in the evening. If you and your partner or flatmates tend to be out at different times in the evening, decide on one day a week when you will all agree to be in and make it a fixed weekly dinner date.

Take it in turns to choose a weekend activity

If your partner or flatmate is a keen gardener, but you are more of a baker, try to take an interest in their hobby and take it in turns to choose an evening or weekend activity that you will both get involved in. You might not have a particular aptitude for propagating plant cuttings, but taking the time to spend a weekend doing something that you know is important to someone else is a great way to build up a relationship. Plus, you might also discover a secret love of gardening, biscuit making or watercolour painting along the way – you never know.

Share music

Taste in music is something that varies wildly from person to person, and you don't have to have identical musical likes and dislikes to be able to live companionably with someone. But it can be fun to spend an evening introducing each other to your favourite new (or old) music and learning to appreciate the tastes of your nearest and dearest. This can make for a pretty lively debate, particularly when it spans generations, but taking the time to find out what makes your partner, child or flatmates tick is always time well spent. This is also a great activity for a wintry Sunday afternoon.

Man's Best Friend

The natural extension of looking after someone other than yourself is to take time to look after a pet, and a number of medical studies have shown the therapeutic benefits of having pets at home. If you would love to have a dog or a cat but aren't currently able to do so – perhaps you live in a rented house or an urban apartment with no outdoor space – there are still ways to get some of the joy and happiness that a furry companion can bring. Here's how.

Offer to look after neighbours' pets

If you know your neighbours are jetting off on holiday, volunteer to look after their pets for them (see page 126). You will be doing a kind deed at the same time as benefiting from spending time with their cats, dogs or goldfish.

> *"A number of medical studies have shown the therapeutic benefits of having pets at home."*

"Borrow" a pet for regular walks

If you aren't able to commit to having a pet at home full-time, there are a number of websites that can connect you with local pet owners who need someone to help take care of their cats and dogs. You fill in your details and get matched with someone in your town or village who needs help looking after their pet, perhaps while they are at work or when they go away at weekends, and you can "borrow" their pet.

Foster a pet

Rescue shelters sometimes need help fostering a pet for a short period of time, while they are waiting to be rehomed. If you think you would like to help out in this way, get in touch with your nearest animal charity and ask about the application process.

10

Unearth Happiness in the Garden

If you have ever stretched out in the gently dappled shade of a tree on a hot summer's afternoon, listening to the bees lazily humming nearby and the rustle of leaves overhead, you won't be surprised to learn that being in contact with nature has the power to make you happier and healthier.

That said, it can be hard to know where to start when it comes to designing and planting up your own patch of garden, especially if you have never picked up a spade before and struggle to identify your annuals from your perennials. To find out how we can all make the most of our outdoor spaces and, more importantly, why we should, I quizzed Professor Alistair Griffiths, Director of Science & Collections at the Royal Horticultural Society (RHS).

"Being in contact with nature has the power to make you happier and healthier."

First up, just what benefits can gardening have for our health and happiness? "I believe that gardens have the power to improve our physical and mental health," says Alistair, "and there is an increasing body of scientific evidence that also proves this...from improved mental health, reduced cardiovascular morbidity and mortality, obesity and risk of type 2 diabetes, to improved pregnancy outcomes and reduced isolation."

Just how can a garden have such a powerful effect? These health benefits are due to the fact that gardens provide "psychological relaxation and stress alleviation, increased physical activity, increased social interaction, reduced exposure to air pollutants, noise and excess heat," he explains.

But do we need to have a large outdoor space to reap the most rewards? Absolutely not, says Alistair. "The key thing is to be out in nature and to get gardening – be it a few houseplants or a large garden."

Three Gardening Activities for Non-gardeners

Ready to dig in? Here are three ways to get going, even if you have never picked up a spade before.

 Start small!
You don't need to have acres of land to become a gardener. In fact, it is often better to start small, as it gives you the freedom to experiment with different plants until you hit on a combination that works for you. "Start with containers or a very small plot of land," recommends Alistair, and choose plants that are easy to grow, such as perennial bulbs that will come up year after year in a container. The more you experiment, the more plants you will find that work well in your climate and you can use those to create the foundation of your garden. "Build on successes and not failures," says Alistair.

② Create a herb garden
Herbs are one of the easiest ways to turn yourself into a gardener, as they are quick, simple and fun to grow. Whether you take over a sunny kitchen windowsill with a few pots or plant up a container outside your kitchen door, choose herbs that you love to cook with and scents that you enjoy. If you plant them outside, use them to line a path or place them close to the front door, so you can brush past them each time you leave the house and release some of that delicious herby scent. The following herbs are all good to start with: rosemary (*Rosmarinus officinalis*); sage (*Salvia officinalis*); chives (*Allium schoenoprasum*); mint (*Mentha*) and basil (*Ocimum basilicum*).

"Choose herbs that you love to cook with and scents that you enjoy."

3 Grow your favourite food

"Food is a great way to get people engaged with gardening," says Alistair, and I have to agree; there is nothing more satisfying than picking your own fresh strawberries in the height of summer. They often taste better than anything you can buy and there is a level of smugness involved when you offer them to friends and family that's hard to beat.

The golden rule with growing fruit or vegetables at home is just to grow whatever you love to eat; it sounds simple but it is easy to get carried away. You could grow a very pretty crop of runner beans for example, because you like the way the delicate scarlet flowers and bright green peapods look as they scramble up a wigwam frame, but if you don't particularly enjoy eating or cooking with green beans then the crop will be wasted and you will run out of enthusiasm for it pretty quickly. Stick instead to growing fruit and vegetables you adore, be that strawberries, tomatoes, lemons or even peppers, and you will create a harvest that's practical as well as pretty. The following are all great crops for non-gardeners to start with.

"The golden rule with growing fruit or vegetables at home is just to grow whatever you love to eat."

Fresh strawberries

These couldn't be simpler to grow. Buy a small plant early in the season – almost any garden centre will sell them – pop it in a container or hanging basket, keep it well watered and wait for your strawberry harvest to arrive in late summer. Invite friends over to share them and practise your casual, "Oh these? I just grew them."

Ripe tomatoes

Again, buy a small plant early in the season and put it in a container or a patch of warm ground to result in a crop of tomatoes in late summer. Or, if you have a warm windowsill and some patience, you can grow your own tomatoes for free, by squeezing the seeds from the centre of a tomato into a pot of compost. With a little care and a dash of luck, these will sprout into tiny shoots, which will turn into small plants, then bigger plants, until they are ready to transfer to the garden in late spring.

"Gold" potatoes

Did you know that if you pop a seed potato into a large bag of compost, it will grow a new crop of delicious potatoes under the surface? I think this is a great trick and it's a good harvest to get children involved in, too, as it's great fun to pull up the leafy plant stems to reveal the little nuggets of potato "gold" below the surface of the compost.

...And one idea for little gardeners

Gardening does take patience, so if you want to get children interested, the key is to choose a plant that is quick to grow and fun to eat. "Try growing seeds that germinate very quickly and which they can eat immediately," Alistair suggests. "Without doubt, cress is a great one for this." Take a clean, hollowed-out eggshell and fill with damp cotton wool. Sprinkle cress seeds carefully onto the cotton wool, then place in a sunny spot and wait for your cress crop to appear!

How to Create an "Outdoor Living Room"

So, now we have ascertained that trees are good, dirt is excellent and being in nature is a balm for the soul, here's how to turn your garden into an outdoor living room to allow you to enjoy those long summer days and nights.

Take your indoor style outside

If you want to relax, unwind and socialize in the garden, you need to think about the space in much the same way as you would an indoor living room, and give equal care to your outdoor décor as you would to your interiors. This means thinking about seating, lighting and accessories. Transform a garden bench into a soft sofa with a few sturdy cushions and blankets, draw up a low table as a handy perch for drinks, snacks and magazines, and bring in colour, pattern and personality with accessories such as lanterns, bunting and oversized floor cushions.

Create some shelter

Don't let inclement weather send you running indoors. Introduce some shelter to your outdoor space, such as a canopy made from sailcloth or a pergola structure, to provide respite from the elements and allow you to stay outside come rain or shine. There's nothing better than listening to the sound of rain gently falling on a canvas roof when you are dry and snug underneath.

"If you want to relax, unwind and socialize in the garden, you need to think about the space in much the same way as you would an indoor living room."

Shed some light

Make your garden an enticing place to linger in the evenings by hanging up a string of twinkling lights or investing in a few garden lanterns to illuminate your outdoor space after dark. Tealights in glass jars or solar-powered string lights are also good options for adding a soft glow. But don't go overboard with the lighting; you don't want to create a floodlit glare, and it's actually detrimental to wildlife to have too much light outside. Stick to soft, romantic lighting for a mellow mood.

Make a fire

A happily crackling fire is lovely to gather around when the evenings draw in, and a small fire pit or chiminea can usually be squeezed into even the most compact outdoor space, as long as there is adequate ventilation. Pop some marshmallows onto a toasting fork, bring out steaming mugs of rich hot chocolate and invite friends and family to share stories around the embers as the scent of wood smoke drifts into the night air. That has to beat a night indoors in front of the TV, doesn't it? It will also allow you to continue using your outdoor space into the autumn months.

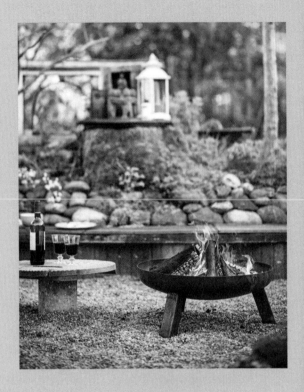

Paint garden fencing, sheds and outbuildings

Most garden fences and sheds are treated with a wood stain in varying shades of brown and given little other consideration. But it is high time we started giving our boundary walls and garden buildings just as much consideration as our indoor walls and furniture. If you update your fencing or shed with a coloured wood stain to complement your interior style, it will help to bring your garden to life and knit your indoor and outdoor spaces together. To help you choose the best shade, think of your garden fencing as a backdrop for your flowers and plants. Dark grey tones will allow bright colours to pop, while lighter shades of grey or white will create the perfect foil for Mediterranean plants such as lavender (*Lavandula*), citrus and olive (*Olea europaea*).

How to Green Up an Urban Garden or Balcony

Don't have acres of outdoor space to garden? Not a problem. Some of the cleverest and most impactful gardens are small urban ones where creativity has to take centre stage. Plus a small garden is much easier to manage. Here's how to squeeze every drop out of your urban garden or balcony and create a mini oasis in the heart of the city.

Grow a green screen

Fast-growing climbers are excellent in a city garden as they can scramble up a boundary wall or fence and provide additional privacy as well as a living green wall to look out on. Bamboo is a good option for a balcony, as it doesn't need a wall to climb up, so it can be planted in a trough and grown up against a railing to provide a soft green screen that will gently rustle and sway in the breeze.

Look up

If floor space is at a premium, you will need to maximize vertical space instead. A wall-hung planter is great for raising flowers off the ground – and this can be anything from a simple hanging basket to a more complex "living wall" arrangement. Plant stands or small tables will also help to raise plant pots up and create a multilayered feel to your outdoor space, making a virtue of a small garden area by creating a lush, cocooning effect.

Create a scent garden

If space is limited in a city garden, go large on scent instead to create a beautiful outdoor space that packs a punch. "Choose scented plants such as lavender (*Lavandula*) and climbers such as jasmine (*Jasminum*) and honeysuckle (*Lonicera*)," suggests Alistair, to turn your outdoor space into a sensory retreat. Be aware that scented plants release their fragrance at different times of the day, too, so if you plan to use the space more in the evenings, choose night-scented plants such as evening primrose (*Oenothera biennis*) for maximum impact.

Start a little tea garden

In a small garden, the plants you choose need to work hard to earn their space. Alistair suggests planting up a little herb garden on a balcony or even in a window box, to provide herbs and plants for making your own fresh tea. Mint (*Mentha*), chamomile (*Matricaria chamomilla*) and lemon balm (*Melissa officinalis*) are good ones to start with.

> *"Many dwarf or compact trees can be suitable for an urban patio or terrace, and some can even be grown in a large pot."*

Squeeze in a tree

Think you haven't got space for a tree? You might be surprised. Many dwarf or compact trees can be suitable for an urban patio or terrace, and some can even be grown in a large pot. I have two dwarf apple trees in my small garden, which are only 1.5m (5ft) tall, but they produce a good crop of full-sized apples in the autumn and an abundance of frothy pink blossom in spring. I also have a dwarf pear tree in the small patch of garden in front of my house, and in the autumn it provides an amazing crop of fruit while in the spring it produces beautiful pure white blossom that drifts down to the ground in a soft confetti of petals. Ask for advice at your local plant nursery to find the right tree for your garden's position and soil type.

Join the Green Gym (It's Free!)

A Harvard Medical School study found that 30 minutes of intense gardening could burn as many calories as 30 minutes of weightlifting, a 30-minute jog or even half an hour of skiing. If you want to get trim while enjoying all the other benefits of being out in the garden, the following activities will all burn calories and help you to shape up. No gym membership fee required!

Good (mild calorie burn)
- Planting seedlings or shrubs
- Raking the lawn
- Bagging up grass or leaves

Better (moderate calorie burn)
- Weeding
- Planting trees
- Mowing the lawn (with an electric or petrol mower)

Best (now you're pumping iron)
- Chopping and splitting wood
- Mowing the lawn with a push mower
- Digging

NATURE IS THE BEST MEDICINE

While a vigorous gardening session will burn calories and get the blood pumping, amazingly, even sitting in a chair and looking out at a green view can have a positive effect on your health. In the 1980s a scientist called Roger S. Ulrich ran an experiment on patients recovering from surgery in hospital and discovered that patients who were able to see trees from their window were discharged from hospital faster, had fewer complications and required less pain medication than those who only had a view of a brick wall.

Go Where the Wild Things Are

Thinking of others rather than ourselves is a proven shortcut to happiness (see pages 118–31). A good way to do this outside is to consider whom you will be sharing your garden with. And by that I don't mean friends and family; I mean the wildlife that will also be making your little patch of oasis their home.

Can looking after wildlife make us happy?

I went back to the RHS to ask Helen Bostock, Senior Horticultural Advisor, if a wildlife-friendly garden could hold the key to happiness outdoors. She believes it can, for three main reasons.

1 "Firstly, there's the simple enjoyment of experiencing nature," says Helen. "A generation which is in danger of suffering 'nature deficit disorder' can be cured with a few hours out in the garden a week, listening to blackbirds or discovering all the insects that a little patch of long grass can hold."

2 Talking of insects, a wildlife garden can also help to keep pests at bay. "By reducing the amount of pesticide used and providing overwintering sites for ladybirds, lacewings and so on, you can increase the number of natural predators in a garden," says Helen, "meaning pests don't get the upper hand."

3 And finally, by creating a wildlife paradise in your back garden, you can do your bit to help support pollinating insects, such as bees and hoverflies, which are essential pollinators of many wildflowers, garden plants, fruit and vegetables. "You can also create a refuge for species such as common frogs or house sparrows that may not be doing so well in the wider countryside," says Helen. Your little bit of garden can act "as an essential patch in a wider green mosaic, making it easier for wildlife to stay connected".

"So, yes, by gardening with wildlife in mind, gardeners reap various rewards," concludes Helen. "And, of course, so does the wildlife."

Helen's tips for creating a wildlife paradise

- Allow a patch of grass to grow long.
- Build a small pond or water feature, ensuring wildlife can readily get in and out of the water.
- Construct a log pile.
- Make a solitary bee hotel or a more elaborate bug hotel.
- Plant a hedge to create a green corridor between you and the neighbours.
- Design a pollinator-friendly border or pot-plant collection, packed with flowers for every month of the year.
- Put up a bat box or bird box.
- Make sure garden lighting is not too bright and doesn't cause light pollution.
- Make a compost heap.

HUG A TREE

Personally, I don't need an excuse to go for a walk in a forest or wood; I have even been known to hug a tree on occasion. But if you need a little encouragement to get outdoors, consider, if you will, the wonderfully named concept of *Shinrin-yoku* or "forest bathing". Japanese scientists have been studying this phenomenon for several years, and they have discovered that spending time walking underneath a cool, leafy canopy can have an astonishingly positive effect on human health, lowering blood pressure, boosting the immune system and reducing stress levels.

While you might not be able to plant a forest in your back garden, the trickle-down effect of being out in any type of nature is hard to dispute. So get out there immediately and find yourself a tree to hug. And if you can't find one, plant one.

11

How to Be Smarter Than Your Smartphone

Much of this book is about the joy of reconnecting with simple pleasures: spending time with friends, savouring a quiet moment in a sunny armchair or enjoying a good night's sleep. In an age when we are increasingly driven by technology, much happiness can be found when we take the time to unplug, disconnect and appreciate the small everyday pleasures of life in the "real world", as opposed to the virtual one.

According to the American Psychological Association's Stress in America survey of 2017, increased usage of social media and constant checking of phones among Americans has led to people feeling increasingly disconnected and more stressed. If you feel like your smartphone use is starting to have a negative impact on your happiness, the following pages will show you how to take charge again.

Take Back Control

That said, I am not advocating a return to a pre-tech era. Far from it. There is so much that is fun, creative and entertaining about the online world. We are better connected than ever before and are able to bring the outside world into our homes in an instant. Online tools can make our lives easier and there is so much to gain from living in a connected world.

Problems can come, however, when the use of gadgets is taken to an extreme, so that our home is no longer a refuge from work, school or outside pressures because we are inviting these things in via our constantly connected phones, tablets and laptops. This can be a particular concern for children or teenagers who struggle to disconnect from the constant chatter of social media, when they should be relaxing in the comfort and security of their family home. However, if you can find a way to embrace tech for everything positive it has to offer and balance it with your offline world, you will be on the right track to happiness.

Be the boss

It's good to review the way you use your devices and social media platforms every now and again, to ensure you are getting the very most out of them while being fully in charge of how you are using them. The key is to get to a point where you are using your phone or tablet for a specific purpose – to read an online magazine, connect with friends or stay updated with news – as opposed to finding yourself at its beck and call.

Take the tech quiz

[Y] [N] Do you constantly check your phone while you are at home?

[Y] [N] Does checking your social media accounts sometimes make you feel stressed or anxious?

[Y] [N] Do you get your work emails directed to your phone and do you check them frequently at home?

[Y] [N] Has your sleep suffered as a result of your phone use?

[Y] [N] Do you ever feel "tired but wired"?

If you answered yes to any of these questions, read on to learn how to embrace tech for all it has to offer while keeping it firmly in balance with other elements of your home life. If you answered no to all of these questions, congratulations – you may skip the next section.

Five Ways to Outsmart Your Smartphone

 Sort your apps

I used to have a lot of apps scattered across my phone's homepage, but when a friend told me about the way she managed and organized the apps on her phone, I thought it was really smart and immediately followed her lead. Here's her secret.

- First, ask yourself if an app is helpful, useful or adds something to your life or wellbeing – this could be a fitness tracking app, a meditation app, your music playlists or a home decorating app, for example. Keep all of these on the front screen of your device so they are easily accessible.
- Next, put all of the apps that you decide are fun, but that you would like to use in moderation, on the second page – these could be your social media accounts, dating apps or news sites, for example.
- And, finally, any apps that have the potential to drain your time without bringing value and positivity to your day (games, gossip sites and so on) get relegated to the last page on your device and, ideally, put into a folder.

That way, each time you check your phone, you will be greeted first by all the apps that help, support and bring joy, and you will be less tempted to idly scroll through those that bring a little less positivity to your life and have the potential to drain your time. It really does help you to get on top of which apps make you happy and which don't.

 Update your notifications

An instant way to take control of your device is to switch off notifications for any apps that are non-essential, such as social media accounts. That way, you can check in with your social media apps or email when you want to, rather than being summoned the second a new message arrives in your inbox. If you still want to receive updates, look at the settings of each individual app – you can usually set them to send you updates just once a day, for example, so decide on a time and frequency that work for you.

3 Be out of office

During your "offline" hours, put an out-of-office notification on all your email accounts, both work and private – even if it's only for a few hours. We are used to doing this when we go on a week-long break, but get into the habit of doing it every time you want to clear some free time outside of work hours. If you want to keep an evening or weekend free for a family event, for example, put an out-of-office notification on your email account to say that you won't be checking in until the next morning, and leave a phone number for any emergencies. This will start to set clear boundaries for those who are likely to contact you during home hours and will put your mind at rest so you can relax and enjoy your downtime.

4 Bring back the telephone table

If you find you are carrying your phone around the house with you and checking it constantly, you might want to ease your dependency a little. Try treating your phone as if it's a landline and always put it back in the same place when you are not using it. A hall table is a good location for this and if you ensure there is a charging cable or docking station set up, it will become second nature to leave your phone there when you walk through the door. That way, you can go and check it whenever you want, but it will start to become a conscious decision rather than a subconscious reflex.

Supercharge your sleep

We all know that we shouldn't check our phones or tablets in bed, but the reality is that many of us do. If you want to cut down on your phone use at bedtime, here are a couple of simple steps to help. Plus three ways that your phone can actually help you to sleep.

- An overload of blue light from digital devices at night-time can play havoc with your sleep patterns (see page 55). If you can't quite bring yourself to banish your phone from the bedroom, switch the screen to night-time mode in the evenings to reduce the levels of blue light.
- Using your smartphone as your alarm clock means it's the first thing you reach for in the morning, and the next logical step is to start checking your email and social media accounts before you've even put a foot out of bed. Get an old-fashioned alarm clock instead and store your phone away from your bed overnight. Choose a fun alarm clock that makes you happy, such as a birdsong alarm or a daylight alarm clock that will gently wake you up by mimicking a sunrise.
- Want to transform your phone from something that robs you of sleep to something that gives it back? Download a sleep app to help soothe you to sleep at night. There are lots

of great sleep apps out there, which you can programme to play soothing sounds or even read you a bedtime story as you drift off, and most will automatically switch off after 30 minutes or so, when you are hopefully sound asleep.

- Want to know exactly how much sleep you are getting each night? Invest in a sleep-tracking wristband to wear overnight and it will track your sleep patterns and download the information onto an app for you to review the next day. This will tell you how many times you woke in the night, as well as logging any patterns of restlessness, which can indicate a problem that you can look at tackling, such as an overheated bedroom or too much surrounding noise.
- If you struggle to switch off the background chatter and worries that race through your mind at night-time, there are a raft of really great guided meditation apps available that you can download to your phone to help you clear some headspace before bedtime.

Reclaim Your Leisure Time

If you find yourself aimlessly scrolling through social media apps or emails before you have even stepped out of bed in the morning and want to break the habit, it can help to think about what you could gain by getting this time back. Rather than spending 20 minutes reading about what the latest reality TV stars are up to, you could use that time to do any of the following instead.

20 minutes in the morning

- Drink a leisurely cup of tea while reading a book in your favourite chair.

- Sit outside feeling the sun on your face as you wake up slowly.

- Spend 20 minutes longer getting ready.

- Listen to a podcast or the radio.

- Have a coffee and a croissant at a café on the way to work, rather than a rushed slice of toast at home.

- Sleep! Enjoy more glorious sleep.

20 minutes in the evening

- Chat on the phone with a friend.

- Potter in the garden.

- Listen to a guided meditation app.

- Read a few chapters of a good book.

- Go for a quick run or bike ride.

- Dedicate the time to a hobby.

MAKE IT FUN
The carrot is always more enticing than the stick, so if you want to impose a daily tech limit for children, try rewarding them with a sticker on a chart each time they stay within the limit you have set – it's a good way to help them work toward something they really want. (This reward system also works for adults.)

Good Idea

Want to dial down the amount of time you and your family spend online at home and reconnect with simple pleasure in the offline world instead? Here's an idea.

Send real mail instead of emails

Why not relearn the joy of letter writing? Coming home to find a letter or small parcel has to be one of the best little pleasures there is. Link up with a friend or relative to send regular post or choose a friend you haven't seen in a while and send them a small parcel out of the blue. This is a great activity for children to get involved with, too.

Here are some suggestions for good (small and light) things to wrap up and send:

For children

- Stickers
- Cheerfully patterned socks
- Pretty hair clips
- Fun stationery
- Paper aeroplane kit
- Small card game
- Small magic trick
- Pins, badges or brooches
- Patches
- Keyring
- Packet of quick-grow vegetable seeds
- Origami paper
- Sunflower seeds (for a sunflower growing contest)
- Small paperback book

For adults

- Sachet of hot chocolate or luxury tea
- Soft, colourful socks
- Paperback book
- Pretty notebook
- Nail polish
- Bar of nice chocolate
- Colourful pens
- Lip balm
- Packet of flower seeds
- Facemask sachet
- Pretty postcard
- Small print to frame

Bibliography and Further Reading

American Psychological Association, "Stress in America: Coping with Change", Stress in America™ Survey, 2017, www.apa.org/news/press/releases/stress /2017/technology-social-media.PDF (accessed 1 August 2017)

bloomon, www.bloomon.co.uk

Carruthers, H. R., Morris, J., Tarrier, N. and Whorwell, P. J., "The Manchester Color Wheel: development of a novel way of identifying color choice and its validation in healthy, anxious and depressed individuals", *BMC Medical Research Methodology*, 2010, 10:12 (Copyright note: © Carruthers et al; licensee BioMed Central Lt. 2010. This article is published under license to BioMed Central Ltd. This is an Open Access article distributed under the terms of the Creative Commons Attribution License (https://creativecommons.org/ licenses/by/2.0/) which permits unrestricted use, distribution, and reproduction in any medium, provided the original work is properly cited.)

Dove, Roja, www.rojadove.com

Farrow & Ball, www.farrow-ball.com

The Fragrance Foundation, fragrancefoundation.org.uk

Hamer, M., Stamatakis, E. and Steptoe, A., "Dose-response relationship between physical activity and mental health: the Scottish Health Survey", *British Journal of Sports Medicine*, 2009, vol. 43, pp.1111–1114

Harvard Medical School, "Calories burned in 30 minutes for people of three different weights", www.health. harvard.edu/diet-and-weight-loss/calories-burned-in-30-minutes-of-leisure-and-routine-activities (accessed 1 August 2017)

Harvard Study of Adult Development, www.adultdevelopmentstudy.org

Haviland-Jones, J., Hale Rosario, H., Wilson, P. and McGuire, T. R., "An Environmental Approach to Positive Emotion: Flowers", *Evolutionary Psychology*, 2005, vol. 3, pp. 104–132

Neom Organics, www.neomorganics.com

Park, S. Q. *et al*, "A neural link between generosity and happiness", *Nature Communications 8*, 2017, No. 15964

The Royal Horticultural Society, www.rhs.org.uk

Saxbe, D.E. and Repetti, R. L., "No Place Like Home: home tours correlate with daily patterns of mood and cortisol", *Personality and Social Psychology Bulletin*, 2010, vol. 36, pp.71–81

Search Inside Yourself, siyli.org

The Sleep Council, sleepcouncil.org.uk

The Sleep Council's Bed Buyer's Guide, www. sleepcouncil.org.uk/wp-content/uploads/2016/11/ BBG-website-view.pdf (accessed 6 December 2017)

Takenaka, K. and Wolverton, B. C., *Plants: Why You Can't Live Without Them*, New Delhi: Roli Books, 2010

Tan, Chade-Meng, *Search Inside Yourself: The Unexpected Path to Achieving Success, Happiness (and World Peace)*, New York: HarperOne, 2012

Ulrich, R. S., "View through a window may influence recovery from surgery", *American Association for the Advancement of Science*, 1984, vol. 224, no. 4647, pp.420–421

Welsh, J., "Smell of Success: Scents Affect Thoughts, Behaviors", www.livescience.com/14635-impression-smell-thoughts-behavior-flowers.html (accessed 7 December 2017)

Wolverton, B. C., *How To Grow Fresh Air: 50 Houseplants that Purify Your Home or Office*, London: Weidenfeld & Nicolson, 2008

Index

Acknowledgements

I would like to say a huge thank you to the team at Octopus for taking me under their wing and turning my spark of an idea into reality; particularly to Stephanie Jackson for understanding my idea right from the start and giving me the go ahead, to the lovely Ella Parsons for her calm editing skills and endless patience, and to the super talented Juliette Norsworthy for weaving her design magic and turning my ideas into a beautiful little gem of a book. I am so grateful to Cathryn Summerhayes at Curtis Brown for putting me in touch with such a talented team.

A huge thank you to all of the scientists, researchers and experts who took time out of their busy schedules to answer my many questions, and for contributing their knowledge and skill to this project. Special thanks are owed to Dr Wolverton, Kozaburo Takenaka, Joa Studholme, Lisa Artis, Nicola Elliott, Roja Dove, Stuart Fenwick, Prof Alistair Griffiths, Dr Phyllis Zee, Kasper Iversen and Helen Bostock; this book couldn't exist without your research, talent and knowledge and it is a privilege to have this opportunity to share your work further.

Debbie Powell's beautiful illustrations bring so much life to this book; I owe you many thanks for each and every one of your bright, joyful little drawings.

Finally, thank you to all my friends and family who have put up with me talking about this book non-stop, for entertaining my endless questions, encouraging me when all the late nights and weekends were starting to overwhelm, and generally being wonderfully, brilliantly supportive. Special thanks to Charlotte Duckworth and Susie Ewert-James, for the knowledge, encouragement, friendship (and wine) you provided along the way.

Picture Credits